THE
MONEY MOON

A Romance

JEFFERY FARNOL

1st WORLD
LIBRARY
Literary Society

The Money Moon

Jeffery Farnol

© 1st World Library, 2006
PO Box 2211
Fairfield, IA 52556
www.1stworldlibrary.com
First Edition

LCCN: 2006936202

Softcover ISBN: 978-1-4218-3066-7
Hardcover ISBN: 978-1-4218-2966-1
eBook ISBN: 978-1-4218-3166-4

Purchase *"The Money Moon"*
as a traditional bound book at:
www.1stWorldLibrary.com/purchase.asp?ISBN=978-1-4218-3066-7

1st World Library is a literary, educational organization
dedicated to:

- Creating a free internet library of downloadable ebooks

- Hosting writing competitions and offering book
publishing scholarships.

Interested in more 1st World Library books?
contact: literacy@1stworldlibrary.com
Check us out at: www.1stworldlibrary.com

1st World Library Literary Society

Giving Back to the World

"If you want to work on the core problem, it's early school literacy."

- James Barksdale, former CEO of Netscape

"No skill is more crucial to the future of a child, or to a democratic and prosperous society, than literacy."

- Los Angeles Times

Literacy... means far more than learning how to read and write... The aim is to transmit... knowledge and promote social participation."

- UNESCO

"Literacy is not a luxury, it is a right and a responsibility. If our world is to meet the challenges of the twenty-first century we must harness the energy and creativity of all our citizens."

- President Bill Clinton

"Parents should be encouraged to read to their children, and teachers should be equipped with all available techniques for teaching literacy, so the varying needs and capacities of individual kids can be taken into account."

- Hugh Mackay

To "JENNIFER"

The One and Only

Whose unswerving FAITH was an Inspiration
Whose GENEROSITY is a bye-word;
This book is dedicated as a mark of GRATITUDE and
AFFECTION

Jeffery Farnol Feb. 10, 1910

CONTENTS

CHAPTER I

*Which, being the first, is, very properly,
the shortest chapter in the book*

When Sylvia Marchmont went to Europe, George Bellew being, at the same time, desirous of testing his newest acquired yacht, followed her, and mutual friends in New York, Newport, and elsewhere, confidently awaited news of their engagement. Great, therefore, was their surprise when they learnt of her approaching marriage to the Duke of Ryde.

Bellew, being young and rich, had many friends, very naturally, who, while they sympathized with his loss, yet agreed among themselves, that, despite Bellew's millions, Sylvia had done vastly well for herself, seeing that a duke is always a duke,—especially in America.

There were, also, divers ladies in New York, Newport, and elsewhere, and celebrated for their palatial homes, their jewels, and their daughters, who were anxious to know how Bellew would comport himself under his disappointment. Some leaned to the idea that he would immediately blow his brains out; others opined that he would promptly set off on another of his exploring expeditions, and get himself torn to pieces by lions and tigers, or devoured by alligators; while others again feared greatly that, in a fit of pique, he would marry some "young person" unknown, and therefore, of course, utterly unworthy.

How far these worthy ladies were right, or wrong in their surmises, they who take the trouble to turn the following pages, shall find out.

CHAPTER II

How George Bellew sought counsel of his Valet

The first intimation Bellew received of the futility of his hopes was the following letter which he received one morning as he sat at breakfast in his chambers in St. James Street, W.

MY DEAR GEORGE—I am writing to tell you that I like you so much that I am quite sure I could never marry you, it would be too ridiculous. Liking, you see George, is not love, is it? Though, personally, I think all that sort of thing went out of fashion with our great-grandmother's hoops, and crinolines. So George, I have decided to marry the Duke of Ryde. The ceremony will take place in three weeks time at St. George's, Hanover Square, and everyone will be there, of course. If you care to come too, so much the better. I won't say that I hope you will forget me, because I don't; but I am sure you will find someone to console you because you are such a dear, good fellow, and so ridiculously rich.

So good-bye, and best wishes,

Ever yours most sincerely,

SYLVIA.

Now under such circumstances, had Bellew sought oblivion and consolation from bottles, or gone headlong to the devil in any of other numerous ways that are more or less inviting, deluded people would have pitied him, and shaken grave heads over him; for it seems that disappointment (more especially in love) may condone many offences, and cover as many sins as Charity.

But Bellew, knowing nothing of that latter-day hysteria which wears the disguise, and calls itself "Temperament," and being only a rather ordinary young man, did nothing of the kind. Having lighted his pipe, and read the letter through again, he rang instead for Baxter, his valet.

Baxter was small, and slight, and dapper as to person, clean-shaven, alert of eye, and soft of movement,—in a word, Baxter was the cream of gentlemen's gentlemen, and the very acme of what a valet should be, from the very precise parting of his glossy hair, to the trim toes of his glossy boots. Baxter as has been said, was his valet, and had been his father's valet, before him, and as to age, might have been thirty, or forty, or fifty, as he stood there beside the table, with one eye-brow raised a trifle higher than the other, waiting for Bellew to speak.

"Baxter."

"Sir?"

"Take a seat."

"Thank you sir." And Baxter sat down, not too near his master, nor too far off, but exactly at the right, and proper distance.

"Baxter, I wish to consult with you."

"As between Master and Servant, sir?"

"As between man and man, Baxter."

"Very good, Mr. George, sir!"

"I should like to hear your opinion, Baxter, as to what is the proper, and most accredited course to adopt when one has been—er—crossed in love?"

"Why sir," began Baxter, slightly wrinkling his smooth brow, "so far as I can call to mind, the courses usually adopted by despairing lovers, are, in number, four."

"Name them, Baxter."

"First, Mr. George, there is what I may term, the Course Retaliatory,—which is Marriage—"

"Marriage?"

"With—another party, sir,—on the principle that there are as good fish in the sea as ever came out, and—er—pebbles on beaches, sir; you understand me, sir?"

"Perfectly, go on."

"Secondly, there is the Army, sir, I have known of a good many enlistments on account of blighted affections, Mr. George, sir; indeed, the Army is very popular."

"Ah?" said Bellew, settling the tobacco in his pipe with the aid of the salt-spoon, "Proceed, Baxter."

"Thirdly, Mr. George, there are those who are content to—to merely disappear."

"Hum!" said Bellew.

"And lastly sir, though it is usually the first,—there is dissipation, Mr. George. Drink, sir,—the consolation of bottles, and—"

"Exactly!" nodded Bellew. "Now Baxter," he pursued, beginning to draw diagrams on the table-cloth with the salt-spoon, "knowing me as you do, what course should you advise me to adopt?"

"You mean, Mr. George,—speaking as between man and man of course,—you mean that you are in the unfortunate position of being—crossed in your affections, sir?"

"Also—heart-broken, Baxter."

"Certainly, sir!"

"Miss Marchmont marries the Duke of Hyde,—in three weeks, Baxter."

"Indeed, sir!"

"You were, I believe, aware of the fact that Miss Marchmont and I were as good as engaged?"

"I had—hem!—gathered as much, sir."

"Then—confound it all, Baxter!—why aren't you surprised?"

"I am quite—over-come, sir!" said Baxter, stooping to recover the salt-spoon which had slipped to the floor.

"Consequently," pursued Bellew, "I am—er—broken-hearted, as I told you—"

"Certainly, sir."

"Crushed, despondent, and utterly hopeless, Baxter, and shall be, henceforth, pursued by the—er—Haunting Spectre of the Might Have Been."

"Very natural, sir, indeed!"

"I could have hoped, Baxter, that, having served me so long,— not to mention my father, you would have shown just a—er shade more feeling in the matter."

"And if you were to ask me,—as between man and man sir,—why I don't show more feeling, then, speaking as the old servant of your respected father, Master George, sir,—I should beg most respectfully to say that regarding the lady in question, her conduct is not in the least surprising, Miss Marchmont being a beauty, and aware of the fact, Master George. Referring to your heart, sir, I am ready to swear that it is not even cracked. And now, sir,—what clothes do you propose to wear this morning?"

"And pray, why should you be so confident of regarding the—er—condition of my heart?"

"Because, sir,—speaking as your father's old servant, Master George, I make bold to say that I don't believe that you have ever been in love, or even know what love is, Master George, sir."

Bellew picked up the salt-spoon, balanced it very carefully upon his finger, and put it down again.

"Nevertheless," said he, shaking his head, "I can see for myself but the dreary perspective of a hopeless future, Baxter, blasted by the Haunting Spectre of the Might Have Been;—I'll trouble you to push the cigarettes a little nearer."

"And now, sir," said Baxter, as he rose to strike, and apply the necessary match, "what suit will you wear to-day?"

"Something in tweeds."

"Tweeds, sir! surely you forget your appointment with the Lady Cecily Prynne, and her party? Lord Mountclair had me on the telephone, last night—"

"Also a good, heavy walking-stick, Baxter, and a knap-sack."

"A knap-sack, sir?"

"I shall set out on a walking tour—in an hour's time."

"Certainly, sir,—where to, sir?"

"I haven't the least idea, Baxter, but I'm going—in an hour. On the whole, of the four courses you describe for one whose life is blighted, whose heart,—I say whose heart, Baxter, is broken,—utterly smashed, and—er—shivered beyond repair, I prefer to disappear—in an hour, Baxter."

"Shall you drive the touring car, sir, or the new racer?"

"I shall walk, Baxter, alone,—in an hour."

CHAPTER III

Which concerns itself with a hay-cart, and a belligerent Waggoner

It was upon a certain August morning that George Bellew shook the dust of London from his feet, and, leaving Chance, or Destiny to direct him, followed a hap-hazard course, careless alike of how, or when, or where; sighing as often, and as heavily as he considered his heart-broken condition required,—which was very often, and very heavily,—yet heeding, for all that, the glory of the sun, and the stir and bustle of the streets about him.

Thus it was that, being careless of his ultimate destination, Fortune condescended to take him under her wing, (if she has one), and guided his steps across the river, into the lovely land of Kent,—that county of gentle hills, and broad, pleasant valleys, of winding streams and shady woods, of rich meadows and smiling pastures, of grassy lanes and fragrant hedgerows,— that most delightful land which has been called, and very rightly, "The Garden of England."

It was thus, as has been said, upon a fair August morning, that Bellew set out on what he termed "a walking tour." The reservation is necessary because Bellew's idea of a walking-tour is original, and quaint. He began very well, for Bellew,—in the morning he walked very nearly five miles, and, in the afternoon, before he was discovered, he accomplished ten more on a hay-cart that happened to be going in his direction.

He had swung himself up among the hay, unobserved by the somnolent driver, and had ridden thus an hour or more in that delicious state between waking, and sleeping, ere the waggoner discovered him, whereupon ensued the following colloquy:

THE WAGGONER. (*Indignantly*) Hallo there! what might you be a doing of in my hay?

BELLEW. (*Drowsily*) Enjoying myself immensely.

THE WAGGONER. (*Growling*) Well, you get out o' that, and sharp about it.

BELLEW. (*Yawning*) Not on your life! No sir,—'not for Cadwallader and all his goats!'

THE WAGGONER. You jest get down out o' my hay,—now come!

BELLEW. (*Sleepily*) Enough, good fellow,—go to!—thy voice offends mine ear!

THE WAGGONER. (*Threateningly*) Ear be blowed! If ye don't get down out o' my hay,—I'll come an' throw ye out.

BELLEW. (*Drowsily*) 'Twould be an act of wanton aggression that likes me not.

THE WAGGONER. (*Dubiously*) Where be ye goin'?

BELLEW. Wherever you like to take me; Thy way shall be my way, and—er—thy people—(Yawn) So drive on, my rustic Jehu, and Heaven's blessings prosper thee!

Saying which, Bellew closed his eyes again, sighed plaintively, and once more composed himself to slumber.

But to drive on, the Waggoner, very evidently, had no mind; instead, flinging the reins upon the backs of his horses, he climbed down from his seat, and spitting on his hands, clenched them into fists and shook them up at the yawning Bellew, one after the other.

"It be enough," said he, "to raise the 'Old Adam' inside o' me to 'ave a tramper o' the roads a-snoring in my hay,—but I ain't a-going to be called names, into the bargain. 'Rusty'—I may be, but I reckon I'm good enough for the likes o' you,—so come on down!" and the Waggoner shook his fists again.

He was a very square man, was this Waggoner, square of head, square of jaw, and square of body, with twinkling blue eyes, and a pleasant, good-natured face; but, just now, the eyes gleamed, and the face was set grimly, and, altogether, he looked a very ugly opponent.

Therefore Bellew sighed again, stretched himself, and, very reluctantly, climbed down out of the hay. No sooner was he fairly in the road, than the Waggoner went for him with a rush, and a whirl of knotted fists. It was very dusty in that particular spot so that it presently rose in a cloud, in the midst of which, the battle raged, fast and furious.

And, in a while, the Waggoner, rising out of the ditch, grinned to see Bellew wiping blood from his face.

"You be no—fool!" panted the Waggoner, mopping his face with the end of his neckerchief. "Leastways—not wi' your fists."

"Why, you are pretty good yourself, if it comes to that," returned Bellew, mopping in his turn. Thus they stood a while stanching their wounds, and gazing upon each other with a mutual, and growing respect.

"Well?" enquired Bellew, when he had recovered his breath somewhat, "shall we begin again, or do you think we have had enough? To be sure, I begin to feel much better for your efforts, you see, exercise is what I most need, just now, on account of the—er—Haunting Spectre of the Might Have Been,—to offset its effect, you know; but it is uncomfortably warm work here, in the sun, isn't it?"

"Ah!" nodded the Waggoner, "it be."

"Then suppose we—er—continue our journey?" said Bellew with his dreamy gaze upon the tempting load of sweet-smelling hay.

"Ah!" nodded the Waggoner again, beginning to roll down his sleeves, "suppose we do; I aren't above giving a lift to a chap as can use 'is fists,—not even if 'e is a vagrant, and a uncommon dusty one at that;—so, if you're in the same mind about it, up you get,—but no more furrin curses, mind!" With which admonition, the Waggoner nodded, grinned, and climbed back to his seat, while Bellew swung himself up into the hay once more.

"Friend," said he, as the waggon creaked upon its way, "Do you smoke?"

"Ah!" nodded the Waggoner.

"Then here are three cigars which you didn't manage to smash just now."

"Cigars! why it ain't often as I gets so far as a cigar, unless it be Squire, or Parson,—cigars, eh!" Saying which, the Waggoner turned and accepted the cigars which he proceeded to stow away in the cavernous interior of his wide-eaved hat, handling them with elaborate care, rather as if they were explosives of a highly dangerous kind.

Meanwhile, George Bellew, American Citizen, and millionaire, lay upon the broad of his back, staring up at the cloudless blue above, and despite heart break, and a certain Haunting Shadow, felt singularly content, which feeling he was at some pains with himself to account for.

"It's the exercise," said he, speaking his thought aloud, as he stretched luxuriously upon his soft, and fragrant couch, "after all, there is nothing like a little exercise."

"That's what they all say!" nodded the Waggoner. "But I notice as them as says it, ain't over fond o' doing of it,—they mostly prefers to lie on their backs, an' talk about it,—like yourself."

"Hum!" said Bellew, "ha! 'Some are born to exercise, some achieve exercise, and some, like myself, have exercise thrust upon them.' But, anyway, it is a very excellent thing,—more especially if one is affected with a—er—broken heart."

"A w'ot?" enquired the Waggoner.

"Blighted affections, then," sighed Bellew, settling himself more comfortably in the hay.

"You aren't 'inting at—love, are ye?" enquired the Waggoner cocking a somewhat sheepish eye at him.

"I was, but, just at present," and here Bellew lowered his voice, "it is a—er—rather painful subject with me,—let us, therefore, talk of something else."

"You don't mean to say as your 'eart's broke, do ye?" enquired the Waggoner in a tone of such vast surprise and disbelief, that Bellew turned, and propped himself on an indignant elbow.

"And why the deuce not?" he retorted, "my heart is no more impervious than anyone else's,—confound it!"

"But," said the Waggoner, "you ain't got the look of a 'eart-broke cove, no more than Squire Cassilis,—which the same I heard telling Miss Anthea as 'is 'eart were broke, no later than yesterday, at two o'clock in the arternoon, as ever was."

"Anthea!" repeated Bellew, blinking drowsily up at the sky

again, "that is a very quaint name, and very pretty."

"Pretty,—ah,—an' so's Miss Anthea!—as a pict'er."

"Oh, really?" yawned Bellew.

"Ah!" nodded the Waggoner, "there ain't a man, in or out o' the parish, from Squire down, as don't think the very same."

But here, the Waggoner's voice tailed off into a meaningless drone that became merged with the creaking of the wheels, the plodding hoof-strokes of the horses, and Bellew fell asleep.

He was awakened by feeling himself shaken lustily, and, sitting up, saw that they had come to where a narrow lane branched off from the high road, and wound away between great trees.

"Yon's your way," nodded the Waggoner, pointing along the high road, "Dapplemere village lies over yonder, 'bout a mile."

"Thank you very much," said Bellew, "but I don't want the village."

"No?" enquired the Waggoner, scratching his head.

"Certainly not," answered Bellew.

"Then—what do ye want?"

"Oh well, I'll just go on lying here, and see what turns up,—so drive on, like the good fellow you are."

"Can't be done!" said the Waggoner.

"Why not?"

"Why, since you ax me—because I don't have to drive no farther. There be the farm-house,—over the up-land yonder, you can't see it because o' the trees, but there it be."

So, Bellew sighed resignedly, and, perforce, climbed down into the road.

"What do I owe you?" he enquired.

"Owe me!" said the Waggoner, staring.

"For the ride, and the—er—very necessary exercise you afforded me."

"Lord!" cried the Waggoner with a sudden, great laugh, "you don't owe me nothin' for that,—not nohow,—I owe you one for a knocking of me into that ditch, back yonder, though, to be sure, I did give ye one or two good 'uns, didn't I?"

"You certainly did!" answered Bellew smiling, and he held out his hand.

"Hey!—what be this?" cried the Waggoner, staring down at the bright five-shilling piece in his palm.

"Well, I rather think it's five shillings," said Bellew. "It's big enough, heaven knows. English money is all O.K., I suppose, but it's confoundedly confusing, and rather heavy to drag around if you happen to have enough of it—"

"Ah!" nodded the Waggoner, "but then nobody never *has* enough of it,—leastways, I never knowed nobody as had. Good-bye, sir! and thankee, and—good luck!" saying which, the Waggoner chirrupped to his horses, slipped the coin into his pocket, nodded, and the waggon creaked and rumbled up the lane.

Bellew strolled along the road, breathing an air fragrant with honey-suckle from the hedges, and full of the song of birds; pausing, now and then, to listen to the blythe carol of a sky-lark, or the rich; sweet notes of a black-bird, and feeling that it was indeed, good to be alive; so that, what with all this,—the springy turf beneath his feet, and the blue expanse over-head, he began to whistle for very joy of it, until, remembering the Haunting Shadow of the Might Have Been, he checked himself, and sighed instead. Presently, turning from the road, he climbed a stile, and followed a narrow path that led away across the meadows, and, as he went, there met him a gentle wind laden with the sweet, warm scent of ripening hops, and fruit.

On he went, and on,—heedless of his direction until the sun grew low, and he grew hungry; wherefore, looking about, he presently espied a nook sheltered from the sun's level rays by a steep bank where flowers bloomed, and ferns grew. Here he sat down, unslinging his knap-sack, and here it was, also, that he first encountered Small Porges.

CHAPTER IV

How Small Porges in looking for a fortune for another, found an Uncle for Himself instead

The meeting of George Bellew and Small Porges, (as he afterward came to be called), was sudden, precipitate, and wholly unexpected; and it befell on this wise:

Bellew had opened his knap-sack, had fished thence cheese, clasp-knife, and a crusty loaf of bread, and, having exerted himself so far, had fallen a thinking or a dreaming, in his characteristic attitude, i.e.:—on the flat of his back, when he was aware of a crash in the hedge above, and then, of something that hurtled past him, all arms and legs, that rolled over two or three times, and eventually brought up in a sitting posture; and, lifting a lazy head, Bellew observed that it was a boy. He was a very diminutive boy with a round head covered with coppery curls, a boy who stared at Bellew out of a pair of very round, blue eyes, while he tenderly cherished a knee, and an elbow. He had been on the brink of tears for a moment, but meeting Bellew's quizzical gaze, he manfully repressed the weakness, and, lifting the small, and somewhat weather-beaten cap that found a precarious perch at the back of his curly head, he gravely wished Bellew "Good afternoon!"

"Well met, my Lord Chesterfield!" nodded Bellew, returning the salute, "are you hurt?"

"Just a bit—on the elbow; but my name's George."

"Why—so is mine!" said Bellew.

"Though they call me 'Georgy-Porgy.'"

"Of course they do," nodded Bellew, "they used to call me the same, once upon a time,—

Georgy Porgy, pudding and pie
Kissed the girls, and made them cry,

though I never did anything of the kind,—one doesn't do that sort of thing when one is young,—and wise, that comes later, and brings its own care, and—er—heart-break." Here Bellew sighed, and hacked a piece from the loaf with the clasp-knife. "Are you hungry, Georgy Porgy?" he enquired, glancing up at the boy who had risen, and was removing some of the soil and dust from his small person with his cap.

"Yes I am."

"Then here is bread, and cheese, and bottled stout,—so fall to, good comrade."

"Thank you, but I've got a piece of bread an' jam in my bundle,—"

"Bundle?"

"I dropped it as I came through the hedge, I'll get it," and as he spoke, he turned, and, climbing up the bank, presently came back with a very small bundle that dangled from the end of a very long stick, and seating himself beside Bellew, he proceeded to open it. There, sure enough, was the bread and jam in question, seemingly a little the worse for wear and tear, for Bellew observed various articles adhering to it, amongst other things, a battered penknife, and a top. These, however, were readily removed, and Georgy Porgy fell to with excellent appetite.

Jeffery Farnol

"And pray," enquired Bellew, after they had munched silently together, some while, "pray where might you be going?"

"I don't know yet," answered Georgy Porgy with a shake of his curls.

"Good again!" exclaimed Bellew, "neither do I."

"Though I've been thinking of Africa," continued his diminutive companion, turning the remain of the bread and jam over and over thoughtfully.

"Africa!" repeated Bellew, staring, "that's quite a goodish step from here."

"Yes," sighed Georgy Porgy, "but, you see, there's gold there, oh, lots of it! they dig it out of the ground with shovels, you know. Old Adam told me all 'bout it; an' it's gold I'm looking for, you see, I'm trying to find a fortune."

"I—er—beg your pardon—?" said Bellew.

"Money, you know," explained Georgy, Porgy with a patient sigh, "pounds, an' shillings, an' bank-notes—in a sack if I can get them."

"And what does such a very small Georgy Porgy want so much money for?"

"Well, it's for my Auntie, you know, so she won't have to sell her house, an' go away from Dapplemere. She was telling me, last night, when I was in bed,—she always comes to tuck me up, you know, an' she told me she was 'fraid we'd have to sell Dapplemere an' go to live somewhere else. So I asked why, an' she said 'cause she hadn't any money,' an' 'Oh Georgy!' she said, 'oh Georgy, if we could only find enough money to pay off the—the—'"

"Mortgage?" suggested Bellew, at a venture.

"Yes,—that's it, but how did you know?"

"Never mind how, go on with your tale, Georgy Porgy."

"If—we could only find enough money, or somebody would leave us a fortune,' she said,—an' she was crying too, 'cause I felt a tear fall on me, you know. So this morning I got up, awful' early, an' made myself a bundle on a stick,—like Dick Whittington had when he left home, an' I started off to find a fortune."

"I see," nodded Bellew.

"But I haven't found anything—yet," said Georgy Porgy, with a long sigh, "I s'pose money takes a lot of looking for, doesn't it?"

"Sometimes," Bellew answered. "And do you live alone with your Auntie then, Georgy Porgy?"

"Yes;—most boys live with their mothers, but that's where I'm different, I don't need one 'cause I've got my Auntie Anthea."

"Anthea!" repeated Bellew, thoughtfully. Hereupon they fell silent, Bellew watching the smoke curl up from his pipe into the warm, still air, and Georgy Porgy watching him with very thoughtful eyes, and a somewhat troubled brow, as if turning over some weighty matter in his mind; at last, he spoke:

"Please," said he, with a sudden diffidence, "where do you live?"

"Live," repeated Bellew, smiling, "under my hat,—here, there, and everywhere, which means—nowhere in particular."

"But I—I mean—where is your home?"

"My home," said Bellew, exhaling a great cloud of smoke, "my home lies beyond the 'bounding billow."

"That sounds an awful' long way off."

"It *is* an awful' long way off."

"An' where do you sleep while—while you're here?"

"Anywhere they'll let me. To-night I shall sleep at some inn, I suppose, if I can find one, if not,—under a hedge, or hay-rick."

"Oh!—haven't you got any home of your own, then,—here?"

"No."

"And—you're not going home just yet,—I mean across the 'bounding billow?'"

"Not yet."

"Then—please—" the small boy's voice was suddenly tremulous and eager, and he laid a little, grimy hand upon Bellew's sleeve, "please—if it isn't too much trouble—would you mind coming with me—to—to help me to find the fortune?—you see, you are so very big, an'—Oh!—will you please?"

George Bellew sat up suddenly, and smiled; Bellew's smile was, at all times, wonderfully pleasant to see, at least, the boy thought so.

"Georgy Porgy," said he, "you can just bet your small life, I will,—and there's my hand on it, old chap." Bellew's lips were solemn now, but all the best of his smile seemed, somehow, to have got into his gray eyes. So the big hand clasped the small one, and as they looked at each other, there sprang up a certain understanding that was to be an enduring bond between them.

"I think," said Bellew, as he lay, and puffed at his pipe again, "I think I'll call you Porges, it's shorter, easier, and I think, altogether apt; I'll be Big Porges, and you shall be Small Porges,—what do you say?"

"Yes, it's lots better than Georgy Porgy," nodded the boy. And so Small Porges he became, thenceforth. "But," said he, after a thoughtful pause, "I think, if you don't mind, I'd rather call you—Uncle Porges. You see, Dick Bennet—the black-smith's boy, has three uncles an' I've only got a single aunt,—so, if you don't mind—"

"Uncle Porges it shall be, now and for ever, Amen!" murmured Bellew.

"An' when d'you s'pose we'd better start?" enquired Small Porges, beginning to re-tie his bundle.

"Start where, nephew?"

"To find the fortune."

"Hum!" said Bellew.

"If we could manage to find some,—even if it was only a very little, it would cheer her up so."

"To be sure it would," said Bellew, and, sitting up, he pitched loaf, cheese, and clasp-knife back into the knap-sack, fastened it, slung it upon his shoulders, and rising, took up his stick.

"Come on, my Porges," said he, "and, whatever you do—keep your 'weather eye' on your uncle."

"Where do you s'pose we'd better look first?" enquired Small Porges, eagerly.

"Why, first, I think we'd better find your Auntie Anthea."

"But,—" began Porges, his face falling.

"But me no buts, my Porges," smiled Bellew, laying his hand upon his new-found nephew's shoulder, "but me no buts, boy, and, as I said before,—just keep your eye on your uncle."

CHAPTER V

How Bellew came to Arcadia

So, they set out together, Big Porges and Small Porges, walking side by side over sun-kissed field and meadow, slowly and thoughtfully, to be sure, for Bellew disliked hurry; often pausing to listen to the music of running waters, or to stare away across the purple valley, for the sun was getting low. And, ever as they went, they talked to one another whole-heartedly as good friends should.

And, from the boy's eager lips, Bellew heard much of "Auntie Anthea," and learned, little by little, something of the brave fight she had made, lonely and unaided, and burdened with ancient debt, to make the farm of Dapplemere pay. Likewise Small Porges spoke learnedly of the condition of the markets, and of the distressing fall in prices in regard to hay, and wheat.

"Old Adam,—he's our man, you know, he says that farming isn't what it was in his young days, 'specially if you happen to be a woman, like my Auntie Anthea, an' he told me yesterday that if he were Auntie he'd give up trying, an' take Mr. Cassilis at his word."

"Cassilis, ah!—And who is Mr. Cassilis?"

"He lives at 'Brampton Court'—a great, big house 'bout a mile from Dapplemere; an' he's always asking my Auntie to marry him, but 'course she won't you know."

"Why not?"

"Well, I think it's 'cause he's got such big, white teeth when he smiles,—an' he's always smiling, you know; but Old Adam says that if he'd been born a woman he'd marry a man all teeth, or no teeth at all, if he had as much money as Mr. Cassilis."

The sun was low in the West as, skirting a wood, they came out upon a grassy lane that presently led them into the great, broad highway.

Now, as they trudged along together, Small Porges with one hand clasped in Bellew's, and the other supporting the bundle on his shoulder, there appeared, galloping towards them a man on a fine black horse, at sight of whom, Porges' clasp tightened, and he drew nearer to Bellew's side.

When he was nearly abreast of them, the horse-man checked his career so suddenly that his animal was thrown back on his haunches.

"Why—Georgy!" he exclaimed.

"Good evening, Mr. Cassilis!" said Small Porges, lifting his cap.

Mr. Cassilis was tall, handsome, well built, and very particular as to dress. Bellew noticed that his teeth were, indeed, very large and white, beneath the small, carefully trained moustache; also his eyes seemed just a trifle too close together, perhaps.

"Why—what in the world have you been up to, boy?" he enquired, regarding Bellew with no very friendly eye. "Your Aunt is worrying herself ill on your account,—what have you been doing with yourself all day?"

Again Bellew felt the small fingers tighten round his, and the small figure shrink a little closer to him, as Small Porges answered,

"I've been with Uncle Porges, Mr. Cassilis."

"With whom?" demanded Mr. Cassilis, more sharply.

"With his Uncle Porges, sir," Bellew rejoined, "a trustworthy person, and very much at your service."

Mr. Cassilis stared, his hand began to stroke and caress his small, black moustache, and he viewed Bellew from his dusty boots up to the crown of his dusty hat, and down again, with supercilious eyes.

"Uncle?" he repeated incredulously.

"Porges," nodded Bellew.

"I wasn't aware," began Mr. Cassilis, "that—er—George was so very fortunate—"

"Baptismal name—George," continued Bellew, "lately of New York, Newport, and—er—other places in America, U.S.A., at present of Nowhere-in-Particular."

"Ah!" said Mr. Cassilis, his eyes seeming to grow a trifle nearer together, "an American Uncle? Still, I was not aware of even that relationship."

"It is a singularly pleasing thought," smiled Bellew, "to know that we may learn something every day,—that one never knows what the day may bring forth; to-morrow, for instance, you also may find yourself a nephew—somewhere or other, though, personally, I—er doubt it, yes, I greatly doubt it; still, one never knows, you know, and while there's life, there's hope. A very good afternoon to you, sir. Come, nephew mine, the evening falls apace, and I grow aweary,—let us on— Excelsior!"

Mr. Cassilis's cheek grew suddenly red, he twirled his moustache angrily, and seemed about to speak, then he smiled instead, and turning his horse, spurred him savagely, and galloped back down the road in a cloud of dust.

"Did you see his teeth, Uncle Porges?"

"I did."

"He only smiles like that when he's awful' angry," said Small Porges shaking his head as the galloping hoof-strokes died away in the distance, "An' what do you s'pose he went back for?"

"Well, Porges, it's in my mind that he has gone back to warn our Auntie Anthea of our coming."

Small Porges sighed, and his feet dragged in the dust.

"Tired, my Porges?"

"Just a bit, you know,—but it isn't that. I was thinking that the day has almost gone, an' I haven't found a bit of the fortune yet."

"Why there's always to-morrow to live for, my Porges."

"Yes, 'course—there's always to-morrow; an' then,—I did find you, you know, Uncle Porges."

"To be sure you did, and an uncle is better than nothing at all, isn't he,—even if he is rather dusty and disreputable of exterior. One doesn't find an uncle every day of one's life, my Porges, no sir!"

"An' you are so nice an' big, you know!" said Porges, viewing Bellew with a bright, approving eye.

"Long, would be a better word, perhaps," suggested Bellew,

smiling down at him.

"An' wide, too!" nodded Small Porges. And, from these two facts he seemed to derive a deal of solid comfort, and satisfaction for he strode on manfully once more.

Leaving the high-road, he guided Bellew by divers winding paths, through corn-fields, and over stiles, until, at length, they were come to an orchard. Such an orchard as surely may only be found in Kent,—where great apple-trees, gnarled, and knotted, shot out huge branches that seemed to twist, and writhe; where were stately pear trees; where peaches, and apricots, ripened against time-worn walls whose red bricks still glowed rosily for all their years; where the air was sweet with the scent of fruit, and fragrant with thyme, and sage, and marjoram; and where the black-birds, bold marauders that they are, piped gloriously all day long. In the midst of this orchard they stopped, and Small Porges rested one hand against the rugged bole of a great, old apple tree.

"This," said he, "is my very own tree, because he's so very big, an' so very, very old,—Adam says he's the oldest tree in the orchard. I call him 'King Arthur' 'cause he is so big, an' strong,—just like a king should be, you know,—an' all the other trees are his Knights of the Round Table."

But Bellew was not looking at "King Arthur" just then; his eyes were turned to where one came towards them through the green,—one surely as tall, and gracious, as proud and beautiful, as Enid, or Guinevere, or any of those lovely ladies, for all her simple gown of blue, and the sunbonnet that shaded the beauty of her face. Yes, as he gazed, Bellew was sure and certain that she who, all unconscious of their presence, came slowly towards them with the red glow of the sunset about her, was handsomer, lovelier, statelier, and altogether more desirable than all the beautiful ladies of King Arthur's court,— or any other court so-ever.

But now Small Porges finding him so silent, and seeing where he looked, must needs behold her too, and gave a sudden, glad cry, and ran out from behind the great bulk of "King Arthur," and she, hearing his voice, turned and ran to meet him, and sank upon her knees before him, and clasped him against her heart, and rejoiced, and wept, and scolded him, all in a breath. Wherefore Bellew, unobserved, as yet in "King Arthur's" shadow, watching the proud head with its wayward curls, (for the sunbonnet had been tossed back upon her shoulders), watching the quick, passionate caress of those slender, brown hands, and listening to the thrilling tenderness of that low, soft voice, felt, all at once, strangely lonely, and friendless, and out of place, very rough and awkward, and very much aware of his dusty person,—felt, indeed, as any other ordinary human might, who had tumbled unexpectedly into Arcadia; therefore he turned, thinking to steal quietly away.

"You see, Auntie, I went out to try an' find a fortune for you," Small Porges was explaining, "an' I looked, an' looked, but I didn't find a bit—"

"My dear, dear, brave Georgy!" said Anthea, and would have kissed him again, but he put her off:

"Wait a minute, please Auntie," he said excitedly, "cause I did find—something,—just as I was growing very tired an' disappointed, I found Uncle Porges—under a hedge, you know."

"Uncle Porges!" said Anthea, starting, "Oh! that must be the man Mr. Cassilis mentioned—"

"So I brought him with me," pursued Small Porges, "an' there he is!" and he pointed triumphantly towards "King Arthur."

Glancing thither, Anthea beheld a tall, dusty figure moving off among the trees.

"Oh,—wait, please!" she called, rising to her feet, and, with Small Porges' hand in hers, approached Bellew who had stopped with his dusty back to them.

"I—I want to thank you for—taking care of my nephew. If you will come up to the house cook shall give you a good meal, and, if you are in need of work, I—I—" her voice faltered uncertainly, and she stopped.

"Thank you!" said Bellew, turning and lifting his hat.

"Oh!—I beg your pardon!" said Anthea.

Now as their eyes met, it seemed to Bellew as though he had lived all his life in expectation of this moment, and he knew that all his life he should never forget this moment. But now, even while he looked at her, he saw her cheeks flush painfully, and her dark eyes grow troubled.

"I beg your pardon!" said she again, "I—I thought—Mr. Cassilis gave me to understand that you were—"

"A very dusty, hungry-looking fellow, perhaps," smiled Bellew, "and he was quite right, you know; the dust you can see for yourself, but the hunger you must take my word for. As for the work, I assure you exercise is precisely what I am looking for."

"But—" said Anthea, and stopped, and tapped the grass nervously with her foot, and twisted one of her bonnet-strings, and meeting Bellew's steady gaze, flushed again, "but you—you are—"

"My Uncle Porges," her nephew chimed in, "an' I brought him home with me 'cause he's going to help me to find a fortune, an' he hasn't got any place to go to 'cause his home's far, far beyond the 'bounding billow,'—so you will let him stay, won't you, Auntie Anthea?"

"Why—Georgy—" she began, but seeing her distressed look, Bellew came to her rescue.

"Pray do, Miss Anthea," said he in his quiet, easy manner. "My name is Bellew," he went on to explain, "I am an American, without family or friends, here, there or anywhere, and with nothing in the world to do but follow the path of the winds. Indeed, I am rather a solitary fellow, at least—I was, until I met my nephew Porges here. Since then, I've been wondering if there would be—er—room for such as I, at Dapplemere?"

"Oh, there would be plenty of room," said Anthea, hesitating, and wrinkling her white brow, for a lodger was something entirely new in her experience.

"As to my character," pursued Bellew, "though something of a vagabond, I am not a rogue,—at least, I hope not, and I could pay—er—four or five pounds a week—"

"Oh!" exclaimed Anthea, with a little gasp.

"If that would be sufficient—"

"It is—a great deal too much!" said Anthea who would have scarcely dared to ask three.

"Pardon me!—but I think not." said Bellew, shaking his head, "you see, I am—er—rather extravagant in my eating,—eggs, you know, lots of 'em, and ham, and beef, and—er—(a duck quacked loudly from the vicinity of a neighbouring pond),— certainly,—an occasional duck! Indeed, five pounds a week would scarcely—"

"Three would be ample!" said Anthea with a little nod of finality.

"Very well," said Bellew, "we'll make it four, and have done with it."

Anthea Devine, being absolute mistress of Dapplemere, was in the habit of exerting her authority, and having her own way in most things; therefore, she glanced up, in some surprise, at this tall, dusty, rather lazy looking personage; and she noticed, even as had Small Porges, that he was indeed very big and wide; she noticed also that, despite the easy courtesy of his manner, and the quizzical light of his gray eyes, his chin was very square, and that, despite his gentle voice, he had the air of one who meant exactly what he said. Nevertheless she was much inclined to take issue with him upon the matter; plainly observing which, Bellew smiled, and shook his head.

"Pray be reasonable," he said in his gentle voice, "if you send me away to some horrible inn or other, it will cost me—being an American, —more than that every week, in tips and things,—so let's shake hands on it, and call it settled," and he held out his hand to her.

Four pounds a week! It would be a veritable God-send just at present, while she was so hard put to it to make both ends meet. Four pounds a week! So Anthea stood, lost in frowning thought until meeting his frank smile, she laughed.

"You are dreadfully persistent!" she said, "and I know it is too much,—but—we'll try to make you as comfortable as we can," and she laid her hand in his.

And thus it was that George Bellew came to Dapplemere in the glory of the after-glow of an August afternoon, breathing the magic air of Arcadia which is, and always has been, of that rare quality warranted to go to the head, sooner, or later.

And thus it was that Small Porges with his bundle on his shoulder, viewed this tall, dusty Uncle with the eye of possession which is oft-times an eye of rapture.

And Anthea? She was busy calculating to a scrupulous nicety the very vexed question as to exactly how far four pounds per week might be made to go to the best possible advantage of all concerned.

CHAPTER VI

Of the sad condition of the Haunting Spectre
of the Might Have Been

Dapplemere Farm House, or "The Manor," as it was still called by many, had been built when Henry the Eighth was King, as the carved inscription above the door testified.

The House of Dapplemere was a place of many gables, and latticed windows, and with tall, slender chimneys shaped, and wrought into things of beauty and delight. It possessed a great, old hall; there were spacious chambers, and broad stairways; there were panelled corridors; sudden flights of steps that led up, or down again, for no apparent reason; there were broad, and generous hearths, and deep window-seats; and everywhere, within, and without, there lurked an indefinable, old-world charm that was the heritage of years.

Storms had buffeted, and tempests had beaten upon it, but all in vain, for, save that the bricks glowed a deeper red where they peeped out beneath the clinging ivy, the old house stood as it had upon that far day when it was fashioned,—in the Year of Our Lord One Thousand Five Hundred and Twenty-four.

In England many such houses are yet to be found, monuments of the "Bad Old Times"—memorials of the "Dark Ages"— when lath and stucco existed not, and the "Jerry-builder" had no being. But where, among them all, might be found such another parlour as this at Dapplemere, with its low, raftered ceiling, its great, carved mantel, its panelled walls whence old portraits looked down at one like dream faces, from dim, and nebulous backgrounds. And where might be found two such bright-eyed, rosy-cheeked, quick-footed, deft-handed Phyllises as the two buxom maids who flitted here and there, obedient to their mistress's word, or gesture. And, lastly, where, in all this wide world, could there ever be found just such another hostess as Miss Anthea, herself? Something of all this was in Bellew's mind as he sat with Small Porges beside him, watching Miss Anthea dispense tea,—brewed as it should be, in an earthen tea-pot.

"Milk and sugar, Mr. Bellew?"

"Thank you!"

"This is blackberry, an' this is raspberry an' red currant—but the blackberry jam's the best, Uncle Porges!"

"Thank you, nephew."

"Now aren't you awful' glad I found you—under that hedge, Uncle Porges?"

"Nephew,—I am!"

"Nephew?" repeated Anthea, glancing at him with raised brows.

"Oh yes!" nodded Bellew, "we adopted each other—at about four o'clock, this afternoon."

"Under a hedge, you know!" added Small Porges.

"Wasn't it a very sudden, and altogether—unheard of proceeding?" Anthea enquired.

"Well, it might have been if it had happened anywhere but in Arcadia."

"What do you mean by Arcadia, Uncle Porges?"

"A place I've been looking for—nearly all my life, nephew. I'll trouble you for the blackberry jam, my Porges."

"Yes, try the blackberry,—Aunt Priscilla made it her very own self."

"You know it's perfectly—ridiculous!" said Anthea, frowning and laughing, both at the same time.

"What is, Miss Anthea?"

"Why that you should be sitting here calling Georgy your nephew, and that I should be pouring out tea for you, quite as a matter of course."

"It seems to me the most delightfully natural thing in the world," said Bellew, in his slow, grave manner.

"But—I've only known you—half an hour—!"

"But then, friendships ripen quickly—in Arcadia."

"I wonder what Aunt Priscilla will have to say about it!"

"Aunt Priscilla?"

"She is our housekeeper,—the dearest, busiest, gentlest little housekeeper in all the world; but with—very sharp eyes, Mr. Bellew. She will either like you very much,—or—not at all! there are no half measures about Aunt Priscilla."

"Now I wonder which it will be," said Bellew, helping himself to more jam.

"Oh, she'll like you, a course!" nodded Small Porges, "I know she'll like you 'cause you're so different to Mr. Cassilis,—he's got black hair, an' a mestache, you know, an' your hair's gold, like mine,—an' your mestache—isn't there, is it? An' I know she doesn't like Mr. Cassilis, an' I don't, either, 'cause—"

"She will be back to-morrow," said Anthea, silencing Small Porges with a gentle touch of her hand, "and we shall be glad, sha'n't we, Georgy? The house is not the same place without her. You see, I am off in the fields all day, as a rule; a farm,—even such a small one as Dapplemere, is a great responsibility, and takes up all one's time—if it is to be made to pay—"

"An' sometimes it doesn't pay at all, you know!" added Small Porges, "an' then Auntie Anthea worries, an' I worry too. Farming isn't what it was in Adam's young days,—so that's why I must find a fortune—early tomorrow morning, you know,—so my Auntie won't have to worry any more—"

Now when he had got thus far, Anthea leaned over, and, taking him by surprise, kissed Small Porges suddenly.

"It was very good, and brave of you, dear," said she in her soft, thrilling voice, "to go out all alone into this big world to try and find a fortune for me!" and here she would have kissed him again but that he reminded her that they were not alone.

"But, Georgy dear,—fortunes are very hard to find,—especially round Dapplemere, I'm afraid!" said she, with a rueful little laugh.

"Yes, that's why I was going to Africa, you know."

"Africa!" she repeated, "Africa!"

"Oh yes," nodded Bellew, "when I met him he was on his way there to bring back gold for you—in a sack."

"Only Uncle Porges said it was a goodish way off, you know, so I 'cided to stay an' find the fortune nearer home."

And thus they talked unaffectedly together until, tea being

over, Anthea volunteered to show Bellew over her small domain, and they went out, all three, into an evening that breathed of roses, and honeysuckle.

And, as they went, slow-footed through the deepening twilight, Small Porges directed Bellew's attention to certain nooks and corners that might be well calculated to conceal the fortune they were to find; while Anthea pointed out to him the beauties of shady wood, of rolling meadow, and winding stream.

But there were other beauties that neither of them thought to call to his attention, but which Bellew noted with observing eyes, none the less:—such, for instance, as the way Anthea had of drooping her shadowy lashes at sudden and unexpected moments; the wistful droop of her warm, red lips, and the sweet, round column of her throat. These, and much beside, Bellew noticed for himself as they walked on together through this midsummer evening.... And so, betimes, Bellew got him to bed, and, though the hour was ridiculously early, yet he fell into a profound slumber, and dreamed of—nothing at all. But, far away upon the road, forgotten, and out of mind,—with futile writhing and grimaces, the Haunting Shadow of the Might Have Been jibbered in the shadows.

CHAPTER VII

Which concerns itself among other matters, with "the Old Adam"

Bellew awakened early next morning, which was an unusual thing for Bellew to do under ordinary circumstances since he was one who held with that poet who has written, somewhere or other, something to the following effect:

"God bless the man who first discovered sleep. But damn the man with curses loud, and deep, who first invented—early rising."

Nevertheless, Bellew, (as has been said), awoke early next morning, to find the sun pouring in at his window, and making a glory all about him. But it was not this that had roused him, he thought as he lay blinking drowsily,—nor the black-bird piping so wonderfully in the apple-tree outside,—a very inquisitive apple-tree that had writhed, and contorted itself most un-naturally in its efforts to peep in at the window;—therefore Bellew fell to wondering, sleepily enough, what it could have been. Presently it came again, the sound,— a very peculiar sound the like of which Bellew had never heard before, which, as he listened, gradually evolved itself into a kind of monotonous chant, intoned by a voice deep, and harsh, yet withal, not unmusical. Now the words of the chant were these:

"When I am dead, diddle, diddle, as well may hap,
Bury me deep, diddle, diddle, under the tap,

Under the tap, diddle, diddle, I'll tell you why,
That I may drink, diddle, diddle, when I am dry."

Hereupon, Bellew rose, and crossing to the open casement leaned out into the golden freshness of the morning. Looking about he presently espied the singer,—one who carried two pails suspended from a yoke upon his shoulders,—a very square man; that is to say, square of shoulder, square of head, and square of jaw, being, in fact, none other than the Waggoner with whom he had fought, and ridden on the previous afternoon; seeing which, Bellew hailed him in cheery greeting. The man glanced up, and, breaking off his song in the middle of a note, stood gazing at Bellew, open-mouthed.

"What,—be that you, sir?" he enquired, at last, and then,— "Lord! an' what be you a doing of up theer?"

"Why, sleeping, of course," answered Bellew.

"W'ot—again!" exclaimed the Waggoner with a grin, "you do be for ever a-sleepin' I do believe!"

"Not when you're anywhere about!" laughed Bellew.

"Was it me as woke ye then?"

"Your singing did."

"My singin'! Lord love ye, an' well it might! My singin' would wake the dead,—leastways so Prudence says, an' she's generally right,—leastways, if she ain't, she's a uncommon good cook, an' that goes a long way wi' most of us. But I don't sing very often unless I be alone, or easy in my mind an' 'appy-'earted,—which I ain't."

"No?" enquired Bellew.

"Not by no manner o' means, I ain't,—contrariwise my 'eart be sore an' full o' gloom,—which ain't to be wondered at, nohow."

"And yet you were singing."

"Aye, for sure I were singin', but then who could help singin' on such a mornin' as this be, an' wi' the black-bird a-piping away in the tree here. Oh! I were singin', I don't go for to deny it, but it's sore 'earted I be, an' filled wi' gloom sir, notwithstanding."

"You mean," said Bellew, becoming suddenly thoughtful, "that you are haunted by the Carking Spectre of the—er Might Have Been?"

"Lord bless you, no sir! This ain't no spectre, nor yet no skellington,—which, arter all, is only old bones an' such,—no this ain't nothin' of that sort, an' no more it ain't a thing as I can stand 'ere a maggin' about wi' a long day's work afore me, axing your pardon, sir." Saying which, the Waggoner nodded suddenly and strode off with his pails clanking cheerily.

Very soon Bellew was shaved, and dressed, and going down stairs he let himself out into the early sunshine, and strolled away towards the farm-yard where cocks crew, cows lowed, ducks quacked, turkeys and geese gobbled and hissed, and where the Waggoner moved to and fro among them all, like a presiding genius.

"I think," said Bellew, as he came up, "I think you must be the Adam I have heard of."

"That be my name, sir."

"Then Adam, fill your pipe," and Bellew extended his pouch, whereupon Adam thanked him, and fishing a small, short, black clay from his pocket, proceeded to fill, and light it.

"Yes sir," he nodded, inhaling the tobacco with much apparent enjoyment, "Adam I were baptized some thirty odd year ago, but I generally calls myself 'Old Adam,'"

"But you're not old, Adam."

"Why, it ain't on account o' my age, ye see sir,—it be all because o' the Old Adam as is inside o' me. Lord love ye! I am nat'rally that full o' the 'Old Adam' as never was. An' 'e's alway a up an' taking of me at the shortest notice. Only t'other day he up an' took me because Job Jagway ('e works for Squire Cassilis, you'll understand sir) because Job Jagway sez as our wheat, (meanin' Miss Anthea's wheat, you'll understand sir) was mouldy; well, the 'Old Adam' up an' took me to that extent, sir, that they 'ad to carry Job Jagway home, arterwards. Which is all on account o' the Old Adam,—me being the mildest chap you ever see, nat'rally,—mild? ah! sucking doves wouldn't be nothin' to me for mildness."

"And what did the Squire have to say about your spoiling his man?"

"Wrote to Miss Anthea, o' course, sir,—he's always writing to Miss Anthea about summat or other,—sez as how he was minded to lock me up for 'sault an' battery, but, out o' respect for her, would let me off, wi' a warning."

"Miss Anthea was worried, I suppose?"

"Worried, sir! 'Oh Adam!' sez she, 'Oh Adam! 'aven't I got enough to bear but you must make it 'arder for me?' An' I see the tears in her eyes while she said it. Me make it 'arder for her! Jest as if I wouldn't make things lighter for 'er if I could,— which I can't; jest as if, to help Miss Anthea, I wouldn't let 'em take me an'—well, never mind what,—only I would!"

"Yes, I'm sure you would," nodded Bellew. "And is the Squire over here at Dapplemere very often, Adam?"

"Why, not so much lately, sir. Last time were yesterday, jest afore Master Georgy come 'ome. I were at work here in the yard, an' Squire comes riding up to me, smiling quite friendly like,—which were pretty good of him, considering as Job

Jagway ain't back to work yet. 'Oh Adam!' sez he, 'so you're 'aving a sale here at Dapplemere, are you?' Meaning sir, a sale of some bits, an' sticks o' furnitur' as Miss Anthea's forced to part wi' to meet some bill or other. 'Summat o' that sir,' says I, making as light of it as I could. 'Why then, Adam,' sez he, 'if Job Jagway should 'appen to come over to buy a few o' the things,—no more fighting!' sez he. An' so he nods, an' smiles, an' off he rides. An' sir, as I watched him go, the 'Old Adam' riz up in me to that extent as it's a mercy I didn't have no pitchfork 'andy."

Bellew, sitting on the shaft of a cart with his back against a rick, listened to this narration with an air of dreamy abstraction, but Adam's quick eyes noticed that despite the unruffled serenity of his brow, his chin seemed rather more prominent than usual.

"So that was why you were feeling gloomy, was it, Adam?"

"Ah! an' enough to make any man feel gloomy, I should think. Miss Anthea's brave enough, but I reckon 'twill come nigh breakin' 'er 'eart to see the old stuff sold, the furnitur' an' that,—so she's goin' to drive over to Cranbrook to be out o' the way while it's a-doin'."

"And when does the sale take place?"

"The Saturday arter next, sir, as ever was," Adam answered. "But—hush,—mum's the word, sir!" he broke off, and winking violently with a side-ways motion of the head, he took up his pitch-fork. Wherefore, glancing round, Bellew saw Anthea coming towards them, fresh and sweet as the morning. Her hands were full of flowers, and she carried her sun-bonnet upon her arm. Here and there a rebellious curl had escaped from its fastenings as though desirous (and very naturally) of kissing the soft oval of her cheek, or the white curve of her neck. And among them Bellew noticed one in particular,—a roguish curl that glowed in the sun with a coppery light, and peeped at him wantonly above her ear.

"Good morning!" said he, rising and, to all appearance, addressing the curl in question, "you are early abroad this morning!"

"Early, Mr. Bellew!—why I've been up hours. I'm generally out at four o'clock on market days; we work hard, and long, at Dapplemere," she answered, giving him her hand with her grave, sweet smile.

"Aye, for sure!" nodded Adam, "but farmin' ain't what it was in my young days!"

"But I think we shall do well with the hops, Adam."

"Ops, Miss Anthea,—lord love you!—there ain't no 'ops nowhere so good as ourn be!"

"They ought to be ready for picking, soon,—do you think sixty people will be enough?"

"Ah!—they'll be more'n enough, Miss Anthea."

"And, Adam—the five-acre field should be mowed today."

"I'll set the men at it right arter breakfast,—I'll 'ave it done, trust me, Miss Anthea."

"I do, Adam,—you know that!" And with a smiling nod she turned away. Now, as Bellew walked on beside her, he felt a strange constraint upon him such as he had never experienced towards any woman before, and the which he was at great pains with himself to account for. Indeed so rapt was he, that he started suddenly to find that she was asking him a question:

"Do you—like Dapplemere, Mr. Bellew?"

"Like it!" he repeated, "like it? Yes indeed!"

"I'm so glad!" she answered, her eyes glowing with pleasure. "It was a much larger property, once,—Look!" and she pointed away across corn-fields and rolling meadow to the distant woods. "In my grandfather's time it was all his—as far as you can see, and farther, but it has dwindled since then, and to-day, my Dapplemere is very small indeed."

"You must be very fond of such a beautiful place."

"Oh, I love it!" she cried passionately, "if ever I had to—give it up,—I think I should—die!" She stopped suddenly, and as though somewhat abashed by this sudden outburst, adding in a lighter tone: "If I seem rather tragic it is because this is the only home I have ever known."

"Well," said Bellew, appearing rather more dreamy than usual, just then, "I have journeyed here and there in this world of ours, I have wandered up and down, and to and fro in it,—like a certain celebrated personage who shall be nameless,—yet I never saw, or dreamed, of any such place as this Dapplemere of yours. It is like Arcadia itself, and only I am out of place. I seem, somehow, to be too common-place, and altogether matter-of-fact."

"I'm sure I'm matter-of-fact enough," she said, with her low, sweet laugh that, Bellew thought, was all too rare.

"You?" said he, and shook his head.

"Well?" she enquired, glancing at him through her wind-tossed curls.

"You are like some fair, and stately lady out of the old romances," he said gravely.

"In a print gown, and with a sun-bonnet!"

"Even so!" he nodded. Here, for no apparent reason, happening to meet his glance, the colour deepened in her cheek and she was silent; wherefore Bellew went on, in his slow, placid tones. "You surely, are the Princess ruling this fair land of Arcadia, and I am the Stranger within your gates. It behoves you, therefore, to be merciful to this Stranger, if only for the sake of—er—our mutual nephew."

Whatever Anthea might have said in answer was cut short by Small Porges himself who came galloping towards them with the sun bright in his curls.

"Oh, Uncle Porges!" he panted as he came up, "I was 'fraid you'd gone away an' left me,—I've been hunting, an' hunting for you ever since I got up."

"No, I haven't gone away yet, my Porges, you see."

"An' you won't go—ever or ever, will you?"

"That," said Bellew, taking the small hand in his, "that is a question that we had better leave to the—er—future, nephew."

"But—why!"

"Well, you see, it doesn't rest with me—altogether, my Porges."

"Then who—" he was beginning, but Anthea's soft voice interrupted him.

"Georgy dear, didn't Prudence send you to tell us that breakfast was ready?"

"Oh yes! I was forgetting,—awfull' silly of me wasn't it! But you are going to stay—Oh a long, long time, aren't you, Uncle Porges?"

"I sincerely Hope so!" answered Bellew. Now as he spoke, his eyes,—by the merest chance in the world, of course,— happened to meet Anthea's, whereupon she turned, and slipped on her sunbonnet which was very natural, for the sun was growing hot already.

"I'm awful' glad!" sighed Small Porges, "an' Auntie's glad too,—aren't you Auntie?"

"Why—of course!" from the depths of the sunbonnet.

"Cause now, you see, there'll be two of us to take care of you. Uncle Porges is so nice an' big, and—wide, isn't he, Auntie?"

"Y-e-s,—Oh Georgy!—what are you talking about?"

"Why I mean I'm rather small to take care of you all by myself alone, Auntie, though I do my best of course. But now that I've found myself a big, tall Uncle Porges,—under the hedge, you know,—we can take care of you together, can't we, Auntie Anthea?"

But Anthea only hurried on without speaking, whereupon Small Porges continued all unheeding:

"You 'member the other night, Auntie, when you were crying, you said you wished you had some one very big, and strong to take care of you—"

"Oh—Georgy!"

Bellew heartily wished that sunbonnets had never been thought of.

"But you did you know, Auntie, an' so that was why I went out an' found my Uncle Porges for you,—so that he—"

But here, Mistress Anthea, for all her pride and stateliness, catching her gown about her, fairly ran on down the path and never paused until she had reached the cool, dim parlour. Being there, she tossed aside her sunbonnet, and looked at herself in the long, old mirror, and,—though surely no mirror made by man, ever reflected a fairer vision of dark-eyed witchery and loveliness, nevertheless Anthea stamped her foot, and frowned at it.

"Oh!" she exclaimed, and then again, "Oh Georgy!" and covered her burning cheeks.

Meanwhile Big Porges, and Small Porges, walking along hand in hand shook their heads solemnly, wondering much upon the capriciousness of aunts, and the waywardness thereof.

"I wonder why she runned away, Uncle Porges?"

"Ah, I wonder!"

"Specks she's a bit angry with me, you know, 'cause I told you she was crying."

"Hum!" said Bellew.

"An Auntie takes an awful lot of looking after!" sighed Small Porges.

"Yes," nodded Bellew, "I suppose so,—especially if she happens to be young, and—er—"

"An' what, Uncle Porges?"

"Beautiful, nephew."

"Oh! Do you think she's—really beautiful?" demanded Small Porges.

"I'm afraid I do," Bellew confessed.

"So does Mr. Cassilis,—I heard him tell her so once—in the orchard."

"Hum!" said Bellew.

"Ah! but you ought to see her when she comes to tuck me up at night, with her hair all down, an' hanging all about her—like a shiny cloak, you know."

"Hum!" said Bellew.

"Please Uncle Porges," said Georgy, turning to look up at him, "what makes you hum so much this morning?"

"I was thinking, my Porges."

"Bout my Auntie Anthea?"

"I do admit the soft impeachment, sir."

"Well, I'm thinking too."

"What is it, old chap?"

"I'm thinking we ought to begin to find that fortune for her after breakfast."

"Why, it isn't quite the right season for fortune hunting, yet—at least, not in Arcadia," answered Bellew, shaking his head.

"Oh!—but why not?"

"Well, the moon isn't right, for one thing."

"The moon!" echoed Small Porges.

"Oh yes,—we must wait for a—er—a Money Moon, you know,—surely you've heard of a Money Moon?"

"Fraid not," sighed Small Porges regretfully, "but—I've heard of a Honey-moon—"

"They're often much the same!" nodded Bellew.

"But when will the Money Moon come, an'—how?"

"I can't exactly say, my Porges, but come it will one of these fine nights. And when it does we shall know that the fortune is close by, and waiting to be found. So, don't worry your small head about it,—just keep your eye on your uncle."

Betimes they came in to breakfast where Anthea awaited them at the head of the table. Then who so demure, so gracious and self-possessed, so sweetly sedate as she. But the Cavalier in the picture above the carved mantel, versed in the ways of the world, and the pretty tricks and wiles of the Beau Sex Feminine, smiled down at Bellew with an expression of such roguish waggery as said plain as words: "We know!" And Bellew, remembering a certain pair of slender ankles that had revealed themselves in their hurried flight, smiled back at the cavalier, and it was all he could do to refrain from winking outright.

CHAPTER VIII

*Which tells of Miss Priscilla, of peaches, and of Sergeant Appleby
late of the 19th Hussars*

Small Porges was at his lessons. He was perched at the great
oak table beside the window, pen in hand, and within easy
reach of Anthea who sat busied with her daily letters and
accounts. Small Porges was laboriously inscribing in a
somewhat splashed and besmeared copy-book the rather
surprising facts that:

A stitch in time, saves nine. 9.

That:

The Tagus, a river in Spain. R.

and that:

Artaxerxes was a king of the Persians. A.

and the like surprising, curious, and interesting items of news,
his pen making not half so many curls, and twists as did his
small, red tongue. As he wrote, he frowned terrifically, and
sighed oft betwixt whiles; and Bellew watching, where he stood
outside the window, noticed that Anthea frowned also, as she
bent over her accounts, and sighed wearily more than once.

It was after a sigh rather more hopeless than usual that,

chancing to raise her eyes they encountered those of the watcher outside, who, seeing himself discovered, smiled, and came to lean in at the open window.

"Won't they balance?" he enquired, with a nod toward the heap of bills, and papers before her.

"Oh yes," she answered with a rueful little smile, "but—on the wrong side, if you know what I mean."

"I know," he nodded, watching how her lashes curled against her cheek.

"If only we had done better with our first crop of wheat!" she sighed.

"Job Jagway said it was mouldy, you know,—that's why Adam punched him in the—"

"Georgy,—go on with your work, sir!"

"Yes, Auntie!" And immediately Small Porges' pen began to scratch, and his tongue to writhe and twist as before.

"I'm building all my hopes, this year, on the hops," said Anthea, sinking her head upon her hand, "if they should fail—"

"Well?" enquired Bellew, with his gaze upon the soft curve of her throat.

"I—daren't think of it!"

"Then don't—let us talk of something else—"

"Yes,—of Aunt Priscilla!" nodded Anthea, "she is in the garden."

"And pray who is Aunt Priscilla?"

"Go and meet her."

"But—"

"Go and find her—in the orchard!" repeated Anthea, "Oh do go, and leave us to our work."

Thus it was that turning obediently into the orchard, and looking about, Bellew presently espied a little, bright-eyed old lady who sat beneath the shadow of "King Arthur" with a rustic table beside her upon which stood a basket of sewing. Now, as he went, he chanced to spy a ball of worsted that had fallen by the way, and stooping, therefore, he picked it up, while she watched him with her quick, bright eyes.

"Good morning, Mr. Bellew!" she said in response to his salutation, "it was nice of you to trouble to pick up an old woman's ball of worsted." As she spoke, she rose, and dropped him a courtesy, and then, as he looked at her again, he saw that despite her words, and despite her white hair, she was much younger, and prettier than he had thought.

"I am Miss Anthea's house-keeper," she went on, "I was away when you arrived, looking after one of Miss Anthea's old ladies,—pray be seated. Miss Anthea,—bless her dear heart!— calls me her aunt, but I'm not really—Oh dear no! I'm no relation at all! But I've lived with her long enough to feel as if I was her aunt, and her uncle, and her father, and her mother— all rolled into one,—though I should be rather small to be so many,—shouldn't I?" and she laughed so gaily, and unaffectedly, that Bellew laughed too.

"I tell you all this," she went on, keeping pace to her flying needle, "because I have taken a fancy to you—on the spot! I always like, or dislike a person—on the spot,—first impressions you know! Y-e-e-s," she continued, glancing up at him side-ways, "I like you just as much as I dislike Mr. Cassilis,—heigho! how I do—detest that man! There, now that's off my mind!"

"And why?" enquired Bellew, smiling.

"Dear me, Mr. Bellew I—how should I know, only I do,—and
what's more—he knows it too! And how," she enquired,
changing the subject abruptly, "how is your bed,—
comfortable, mm?"

"Very!"

"You sleep well?"

"Like a top!"

"Any complaints, so far?"

"None whatever," laughed Bellew, shaking his head.

"That is very well. We have never had a boarder before, and
Miss Anthea,—bless her dear soul! was a little nervous about it.
And here's the Sergeant!"

"I—er—beg your pardon—?" said Bellew.

"The Sergeant!" repeated Miss Priscilla, with a prim little nod,
"Sergeant Appleby, late of the Nineteenth Hussars,—a soldier
every inch of him, Mr. Bellew,—with one arm—over there by
the peaches." Glancing in the direction she indicated, Bellew
observed a tall figure, very straight and upright, clad in a tight-
fitting blue coat, with extremely tight trousers strapped
beneath the insteps, and with a hat balanced upon his close-
cropped, grizzled head at a perfectly impossible angle for any
save an ex-cavalry-man. Now as he stood examining a peach-
tree that flourished against the opposite wall, Bellew saw that
his right sleeve was empty, sure enough, and was looped across
his broad chest.

"The very first thing he will say will be that 'it is a very fine
day,'" nodded Miss Priscilla, stitching away faster than ever,
"and the next, that 'the peaches are doing remarkably well,'—

now mark my words, Mr. Bellew." As she spoke, the Sergeant wheeled suddenly right about face, and came striding down towards them, jingling imaginary spurs, and with his stick tucked up under his remaining arm, very much as if it had been a sabre.

Being come up to them, the Sergeant raised a stiff arm as though about to salute them, military fashion, but, apparently changing his mind, took off the straw hat instead, and put it on again, more over one ear than ever.

"A particular fine day, Miss Priscilla, for the time o' the year," said he.

"Indeed I quite agree with you Sergeant," returned little Miss Priscilla with a bright nod, and a sly glance at Bellew, as much as to say, "I told you so!" "And the peaches, mam," continued the Sergeant, "the peaches—never looked—better, mam." Having said which, he stood looking at nothing in particular, with his one hand resting lightly upon his hip.

"Yes, to be sure, Sergeant," nodded Miss Priscilla, with another sly look. "But let me introduce you to Mr. Bellew who is staying at Dapplemere." The Sergeant stiffened, once more began a salute, changed his mind, took off his hat instead, and, after looking at it as though not quite sure what to do with it next, clapped it back upon his ear, in imminent danger of falling off, and was done with it.

"Proud to know you, sir,—your servant, sir!"

"How do you do!" said Bellew, and held out his hand with his frank smile. The Sergeant hesitated, then put out his remaining hand.

"My left, sir," said he apologetically, "can't be helped—left my right—out in India—a good many years ago. Good place for soldiering, India, sir—plenty of active service—chances of promotion—though sun bad!"

"Sergeant," said Miss Priscilla, without seeming to glance up from her sewing, "Sergeant,—your hat!" Hereupon, the Sergeant gave a sudden, sideways jerk of the head, and, in the very nick of time, saved the article in question from tumbling off, and very dexterously brought it to the top of his close-cropped head, whence it immediately began, slowly, and by scarcely perceptible degrees to slide down to his ear again.

"Sergeant," said Miss Priscilla again, "sit down,—do."

"Thank you mam," said he, and proceeded to seat himself at the other end of the rustic bench, where he remained, bolt upright, and with his long legs stretched out straight before him, as is, and has been, the manner of cavalrymen since they first wore straps.

"And now," said he, staring straight in front of him, "how might Miss Anthea be?"

"Oh, very well, thank you," nodded Miss Priscilla.

"Good!" exclaimed the Sergeant, with his eyes still fixed, "very good!" Here he passed his hand two or three times across his shaven chin, regarding an apple-tree, nearby, with an expression of the most profound interest:

"And how," said he again, "how might Master Georgy be?"

"Master Georgy is as well as ever," answered Miss Priscilla, stitching away faster than before, and Bellew thought she kept her rosy cheeks stooped a little lower over her work. Meanwhile the Sergeant continued to regard the tree with the same degree of lively interest, and to rasp his fingers to and fro across his chin. Suddenly, he coughed behind hand, whereupon Miss Priscilla raised her head, and looked at him.

"Well?" she enquired, very softly:

"And pray, mam," said the Sergeant, removing his gaze from

the tree with a jerk, "how might—you be feeling, mam?"

"Much the same as usual, thank you," she answered, smiling like a girl, for all her white hair, as the Sergeant's eyes met hers.

"You look," said he, pausing to cough behind his hand again, "you look—blooming, mam,—if you'll allow the expression, —blooming,—as you ever do, mam."

"I'm an old woman, Sergeant, as well you know!" sighed Miss Priscilla, shaking her head.

"Old, mam!" repeated the Sergeant, "old, mam!—nothing of the sort, mam!—Age has nothing to do with it.—'Tisn't the years as count.—We aren't any older than we feel,—eh, sir?"

"Of course not!" answered Bellew.

"Nor than we look,—eh sir?"

"Certainly not, Sergeant!" answered Bellew.

"And she, sir,—she don't look—a day older than—"

"Thirty five!" said Bellew.

"Exactly, sir, very true! My own opinion,—thirty five exactly, sir."

"Sergeant," said Miss Priscilla, bending over her work again, "Sergeant,—your hat!" The Sergeant, hereupon, removed the distracting head-gear altogether, and sat with it upon his knee, staring hard at the tree again. Then, all at once, with a sudden gesture he drew a large, silver watch from his pocket,—rather as if it were some weapon of offence,—looked at it, listened to it, and then nodding his head, rose to his feet.

"Must be going," he said, standing very straight, and looking down at little Miss Priscilla, "though sorry, as ever,—must be going, mam,—Miss Priscilla mam—good day to you!" And he stretched out his hand to her with a sudden, jerky movement. Miss Priscilla paused in her sewing, and looked up at him with her youthful smile:

"Must you go—so soon, Sergeant? Then Good-bye,—until to-morrow," and she laid her very small hand in his big palm. The Sergeant stared down at it as though he were greatly minded to raise it to his lips, instead of doing which, he dropped it, suddenly, and turned to Bellew:

"Sir, I am—proud to have met you. Sir, there is a poor crippled soldier as I know,—My cottage is very small, and humble sir, but if you ever feel like—dropping in on him, sir,—by day or night, he will be—honoured, sir, honoured! And that's me—Sergeant Richard Appleby—late of the Nineteenth Hussars—at your service, sir!" saying which, he put on his hat, stiff-armed, wheeled, and strode away through the orchard, jingling his imaginary spurs louder than ever.

"Well?" enquired Miss Priscilla in her quick, bright way, "Well Mr. Bellew, what do you think of him?—first impressions are always best,—at least, I think so,—what do you think of Sergeant Appleby?"

"I think he's a splendid fellow," said Bellew, looking after the Sergeant's upright figure.

"A very foolish old fellow, I think, and as stiff as one of the ram-rods of one of his own guns!" said Miss Priscilla, but her clear, blue eyes were very soft, and tender as she spoke.

"And as fine a soldier as a man, I'm sure," said Bellew.

"Why yes, he *was* a good soldier, once upon a time, I believe,—he won the Victoria Cross for doing something or other that was very brave, and he wears it with all his other medals, pinned on the inside of his coat. Oh yes, he was a fine soldier, once, but he's a very foolish old soldier, now,—I think, and as stiff as the ram-rod of one of his own guns. But I'm glad you like him, Mr. Bellew, and he will be proud, and happy for you to call and see him at his cottage. And now, I suppose, it is half past eleven, isn't it?"

"Yes, just half past!" nodded Bellew, glancing at his watch.

"Exact to time, as usual!" said Miss Priscilla, "I don't think the Sergeant has missed a minute, or varied a minute in the last five years,—you see, he is such a very methodical man, Mr. Bellew!"

"Why then, does he come every day, at the same hour?"

"Every day!" nodded Miss Priscilla, "it has become a matter of habit with him."

"Ah?" said Bellew, smiling.

"If you were to ask me why he comes, I should answer that I fancy it is to—look at the peaches. Dear me, Mr. Bellew! what a very foolish old soldier he is, to be sure!" Saying which, pretty, bright-eyed Miss Priscilla, laughed again, folded up her work, settled it in the basket with a deft little pat, and, rising, took a small, crutch stick from where it had lain concealed, and then, Bellew saw that she was lame.

"Oh yes,—I'm a cripple, you see," she nodded,—"Oh very, very lame! My ankle, you know. That is why I came here, the big world didn't want a poor, lame, old woman,—that is why Miss Anthea made me her Aunt, God bless her! No thank you,—I can carry my basket. So you see,—he—has lost an arm,—his right one, and I—am lame in my foot. Perhaps that is why—Heigho! how beautifully the black birds are singing this morning, to be sure!"

CHAPTER IX

*In which may be found some description of
Arcadia, and gooseberries*

Anthea, leaning on her rake in a shady corner of the five-acre
field, turned to watch Bellew who, stripped to his shirt-sleeves,
bare of neck, and arm, and pitch-fork in hand, was busy
tossing up great mounds of sweet-smelling hay to Adam who
stood upon a waggon to receive it, with Small Porges perched
up beside him.

A week had elapsed since Bellew had found his way to
Dapplemere, a week which had only served to strengthen the
bonds of affection between him and his "nephew," and to win
over sharp-eyed, shrewd little Miss Priscilla to the extent of
declaring him to be: "First a gentleman, Anthea, my dear, and
Secondly,—what is much rarer, now-a-days,—a true man!" A
week! and already he was hail-fellow-well-met with everyone
about the place, for who was proof against his unaffected
gaiety, his simple, easy, good-fellowship? So he laughed, and
joked as he swung his pitch-fork, (awkwardly enough, to be
sure), and received all hints, and directions as to its use, in the
kindly spirit they were tendered. And Anthea, watching him
from her shady corner, sighed once or twice, and catching
herself, so doing, stamped her foot at herself, and pulled her
sunbonnet closer about her face.

"No, Adam," he was saying, "depend upon it, there is nothing
like exercise, and, of all exercise,—give me a pitch-fork."

"Why, as to that, Mr. Belloo, sir," Adam retorted, "I say—so be it, so long as I ain't near the wrong end of it, for the way you do 'ave of flourishin' an' a whirlin' that theer fork, is fair as-tonishin', I do declare it be."

"Why you see, Adam, there are some born with a leaning towards pitch-forks, as there are others born to the pen, and the—er—palette, and things, but for me, Adam, the pitch-fork, every time!" said Bellew, mopping his brow.

"If you was to try an' 'andle it more as if it *was* a pitchfork now, Mr. Belloo, sir—" suggested Adam, and, not waiting for Bellew's laughing rejoinder, he chirruped to the horses, and the great waggon creaked away with its mountainous load, surmounted by Adam's grinning visage, and Small Porges' golden curls, and followed by the rest of the merry-voiced hay-makers.

Now it was, that turning his head, Bellew espied Anthea watching him, whereupon he shouldered his fork, and coming to where she sat upon a throne of hay, he sank down at her feet with a luxurious sigh. She had never seen him without a collar, before, and now she could not but notice how round, and white, and powerful his neck was, and how the muscles bulged upon arm, and shoulder, and how his hair curled in small, damp rings upon his brow.

"It is good," said he, looking up into the witching face, above him, "yes, it is very good to see you idle—just for once."

"And I was thinking it was good to see you work,—just for once."

"Work!" he exclaimed, "my dear Miss Anthea, I assure you I have become a positive glutton for work. It has become my earnest desire to plant things, and grow things, and chop things with axes; to mow things with scythes. I dream of pastures, and ploughs, of pails and pitchforks, by night; and, by day, reaping-hooks, hoes, and rakes, are in my thoughts continually,—which all goes to show the effect of this wonderful air of Arcadia. Indeed, I am as full of suppressed energy, these days, as Adam is of the 'Old Adam.' And, talking of Adam reminds me that he has solemnly pledged himself to initiate me into the mysteries of swinging a scythe to-morrow morning at—five o'clock! Yes indeed, my heart bounds responsive to the swish of a scythe in thick grass, and my soul sits enraptured upon a pitch-fork."

"How ridiculous you are!" she laughed.

"And how perfectly content!" he added.

"Is anyone ever quite content?" she sighed, glancing down at him, wistful-eyed.

"Not unless they have found Arcadia," he answered.

"Have you then?"

"Yes," he nodded complacently, "oh yes, I've found it."

"Are you—sure?"

"Quite sure!"

"Arcadia!" she repeated, wrinkling her brows, "what is Arcadia and—where?"

"Arcadia," answered Bellew, watching the smoke rise up from his pipe, with a dreamy eye, "Arcadia is the—Promised Land,—the Land that everyone tries to find, sometime or other, and may be—anywhere."

"And how came you to—find it?"

"By the most fortunate chance in the world."

"Tell me," said Anthea, taking a wisp of hay, and beginning to plait it in dexterous, brown fingers, "tell me how you found it."

"Why then you must know, in the first place," he began in his slow, even voice, "that it is a place I have sought for in all my wanderings, and I have been pretty far afield,—but I sought it so long, and so vainly, that I began to think it was like the El Dorado of the old Adventurers, and had never existed at all."

"Yes?" said Anthea, busy with her plaiting.

"But, one day,—Fate, or Chance, or Destiny,—or their benevolent spirit, sent a certain square-shouldered Waggoner to show me the way, and, after him, a very small Porges, —bless him!—to lead me into this wonderful Arcadia."

"Oh, I see!" nodded Anthea, very intent upon her plaiting.

"But there is something more," said Bellew.

"Oh?" said Anthea.

"Shall I tell you?"

"If—it is—very interesting."

"Well then, in this delightful land there is a castle, grim, embattled, and very strong."

"A castle?" said Anthea, glancing up suddenly.

"The Castle of Heart's Desire."

"Oh!" said she, and gave all her attention to her plaiting again.

"And so," continued Bellew, "I am waiting, very patiently, until, in her own good time, she who rules within, shall open the gate to me, or—bid me go away."

Into Bellew's voice had crept a thrill no one had ever heard there before; he leaned nearer to her, and his dreamy eyes were keen now, and eager. And she, though she saw nothing of all this, yet, being a woman, knew it was there, of course, and, for that very reason, looked resolutely away. Wherefore, once again, Bellew heartily wished that sunbonnets had never been invented.

So there was silence while Anthea stared away across the golden corn-fields, yet saw nothing of them, and Bellew looked upon those slender, capable fingers, that had faltered in their plaiting and stopped. And thus, upon the silence there broke a sudden voice shrill with interest:

"Go on, Uncle Porges,—what about the dragons? Oh, please go on!—there's always dragons in 'chanted castles, you know, to guard the lovely Princess,—aren't you going to have any dragons that hiss, you know, an' spit out smoke, an' flames? Oh!—do please have a dragon." And Small Porges appeared from the other side of the hay-mow, flushed, and eager.

"Certainly, my Porges," nodded Bellew, drawing the small figure down beside him, "I was forgetting the dragons, but there they are, with scaly backs, and iron claws, spitting out sparks and flames, just as self-respecting dragons should, and roaring away like thunder."

"Ah!" exclaimed Small Porges, nestling closer to Bellew, and reaching out a hand to Auntie Anthea, "that's fine! let's have plenty of dragons."

"Do you think a—er—dozen would be enough, my Porges?"

"Oh yes! But s'pose the beautiful Princess didn't open the door,—what would you do if you were really a wandering knight who was waiting patiently for it to open,—what would you do then?"

"Shin up a tree, my Porges."

"Oh but that wouldn't be a bit right—would it, Auntie?"

"Of course not!" laughed Anthea, "it would be most un-knight-like, and very undignified."

"Sides," added Small Porges, "you couldn't climb up a tree in your armour, you know."

"Then I'd make an awful' good try at it!" nodded Bellew.

"No," said Small Porges, shaking his head, "shall I tell you what you ought to do? Well then, you'd draw your two-edged sword, an' dress your shield,—like Gareth, the Kitchen Knave did,—he was always dressing his shield, an' so was Lancelot, —an' you'd fight all those dragons, an' kill them, an' cut their heads off."

"And then what would happen?" enquired Bellew.

"Why then the lovely Princess would open the gate, an' marry you of course, an' live happy ever after, an' all would be revelry an' joy."

"Ah!" sighed Bellew, "if she'd do that, I think I'd fight all the dragons that ever roared,—and kill them too. But supposing she—er—wouldn't open the gate."

"Why then," said Small Porges, wrinkling his brow, "why then—you'd have to storm the castle, of course, an' break open the gate an' run off with the Princess on your charger,—if she was very beautiful, you know."

"A most excellent idea, my Porges! If I should happen to find myself in like circumstances, I'll surely take your advice."

Now, as he spoke, Bellew glanced at Anthea, and she at him. And straightway she blushed, and then she laughed, and then she blushed again, and, still blushing, rose to her feet, and turned to find Mr. Cassilis within a yard of them.

"Ah, Miss Anthea," said he, lifting his hat, "I sent Georgy to find you, but it seems he forgot to mention that I was waiting."

"I'm awful' sorry, Mr. Cassilis,—but Uncle Porges was telling us 'bout dragons, you know," Small Porges hastened to explain.

"Dragons!" repeated Mr. Cassilis, with his supercilious smile, "ah, indeed! dragons should be interesting, especially in such a very quiet, shady nook as this,—quite an idyllic place for story-telling, it's a positive shame to disturb you," and his sharp, white teeth gleamed beneath his moustache, as he spoke, and he tapped his riding-boot lightly with his hunting-crop as he fronted Bellew, who had risen, and stood bare-armed, leaning upon his pitch-fork. And, as in their first meeting, there was a mute antagonism in their look.

"Let me introduce you to each other," said Anthea, conscious of this attitude,—"Mr. Cassilis, of Brampton Court,—Mr. Bellew!"

"Of nowhere in particular, sir!" added Bellew.

"And pray," said Mr. Cassilis perfunctorily as they strolled on across the meadow, "how do you like Dapplemere, Mr. Bellew?"

"Immensely, sir,—beyond all expression!"

"Yes, it is considered rather pretty, I believe."

"Lovely, sir!" nodded Bellew, "though it is not so much the beauty of the place itself, that appeals to me so much as what it—contains."

"Oh, indeed!" said Mr. Cassilis, with a sudden, sharp glance, "to what do you refer?"

"Goose-berries, sir!"

"I—ah—beg your pardon?"

"Sir," said Bellew gravely, "all my life I have fostered a secret passion for goose-berries—raw, or cooked,—in pie, pudding or jam, they are equally alluring. Unhappily the American goose-berry is but a hollow mockery, at best—"

"Ha?" said Mr. Cassilis, dubiously.

"Now, in goose-berries, as in everything else, sir, there is to be found the superlative, the quintessence,—the ideal. Consequently I have roamed East and West, and North and South, in quest of it."

"Really?" said Mr. Cassilis, stifling a yawn, and turning towards Miss Anthea with the very slightest shrug of his shoulders.

"And, in Dapplemere," concluded Bellew, solemnly, "I have, at last, found my ideal—"

"Goose-berry!" added Anthea with a laugh in her eyes.

"Arcadia being a land of ideals!" nodded Bellew.

"Ideals," said Mr. Cassilis, caressing his moustache, "ideals and—ah—goose-berries,—though probably excellent things in themselves, are apt to pall upon one, in time; personally, I find them equally insipid,—"

"Of course it is all a matter of taste!" sighed Bellew.

"But," Mr. Cassilis went on, fairly turning his back upon him, "the subject I wished to discuss with you, Miss Anthea, was the—er —approaching sale."

"The sale!" she repeated, all the brightness dying out of her face.

"I wished," said Cassilis, leaning nearer to her, and lowering his voice confidentially, "to try to convince you how—unnecessary it would be—if—" and he paused, significantly.

Anthea turned quickly aside, as though to hide her mortification from Bellew's keen eyes; whereupon he, seeing it all, became, straightway, more dreamy than ever, and, laying a hand upon Small Porges' shoulder, pointed with his pitch-fork to where at the other end of the "Five-acre" the hay-makers worked away as merrily as ever:

"Come, my Porges," said he, "let us away and join yon happy throng, and—er—

'With Daphnis, and Clo, and Blowsabel
We'll list to the—er—cuckoo in the dell.'

So, hand in hand, the two Porges set off together. But when they had gone some distance, Bellew looked back, and then he saw that Anthea walked with her head averted, yet Cassilis walked close beside her, and stooped, now and then, until the black moustache came very near the curl—that curl of wanton witchery that peeped above her ear.

"Uncle Porges—why do you frown so?"

"Frown, my Porges,—did I? Well, I was thinking."

"Well, I'm thinking too, only I don't frown, you know, but I'm thinking just the same."

"And what might you be thinking, nephew?"

"Why I was thinking that although you're so awful fond of goose-berries, an' though there's lots of ripe ones on the bushes I've never seen you eat a single one."

CHAPTER X

How Bellew and Adam entered into a solemn league and covenant

"Look at the moon to-night, Uncle Porges!"

"I see it."

"It's awfull' big, an' round, isn't it?"

"Yes, it's very big, and very round."

"An'—rather—yellow, isn't it?"

"Very yellow!"

"Just like a great, big golden sovereign, isn't it"

"Very much like a sovereign, my Porges."

"Well, do you know, I was wondering—if there was any chance that it was a—Money Moon?"

They were leaning out at the lattice, Small Porges, and Big Porges. Anthea and Miss Priscilla were busied upon household matters wholly feminine, wherefore Small Porges had drawn Bellew to the window, and there they leaned, the small body enfolded by Bellew's long arm, and the two faces turned up to the silvery splendour of the moon.

Jeffery Farnol

But now, Anthea came up behind them, and, not noticing the position of Bellew's arm as she leaned on the other side of Small Porges, it befell that her hand touched, and for a moment, rested upon Bellew's hand, hidden as it was in the shadow. And this probably began it.

The air of Arcadia, as has been said before, is an intoxicating air; but it is more, it is an air charged with a subtle magic whereby the commonest objects, losing their prosaic, matter-of-fact shapes, become transfigured into things of wonder, and delight. Little things that pass as mere ordinary common-places,—things insignificant, and wholly beneath notice in the every day world, become fraught with such infinite meaning, and may hold such sublime, such undreamed of possibilities —here in Arcadia. Thus, when it is recorded that Anthea's hand accidentally touched, and rested upon Bellew's—the significance of it will become at once apparent.

"And pray," said Anthea, laying that same hand in the most natural manner in the world, upon the Small Porges' curls, "Pray what might you two be discussing so very solemnly?"

"The moon," answered Small Porges. "I was wondering if it was a Money Moon, an' Uncle Porges hasn't said if it is, yet."

"Why no, old chap," answered Bellew, "I'm afraid not."

"And pray," said Anthea again, "what might a Money Moon be?"

"Well," explained Small Porges, "when the moon's just—just so, then you go out an'—an' find a fortune, you know. But the moon's got to be a Money Moon, and you've got to know, you know, else you'll find nothing, of course."

"Ah Georgy dear!" sighed Anthea, stooping her dark head down to his golden curls, "don't you know that fortunes are very hard to get, and that they have to be worked for, and that no one ever found one without a great deal of labour, and sorrow?"

"Course—everyone can't find fortunes, Auntie Anthea, I know that, but we shall,—my Uncle Porges knows all about it, you see, an' I know that we shall. I'm sure as sure we shall find one, some day, 'cause, you see, I put it in my prayers now,—at the end, you know. I say: 'An' please help me an' my Uncle Porges to find a fortune when the Money Moon comes,—a big one, world without end—Amen!' So you see, it's all right, an' we're just waiting till the Money Moon comes, aren't we, Uncle Porges?"

"Yes, old chap, yes," nodded Bellew, "until the Money Moon comes."

And so there fell a silence between them, yet a silence that held a wondrous charm of its own; a silence that lasted so long that the coppery curls drooped lower, and lower upon Bellew's arm, until Anthea, sighing, rose, and in a very tender voice bade Small Porges say 'Goodnight!' the which he did, forthwith, slumberous of voice, and sleepy eyed, and so, with his hand in Anthea's, went drowsily up to bed.

Wherefore, seeing that Miss Priscilla had bustled away into the kitchen, Bellew sauntered out into the rose-garden to look upon the beauty of the night. The warm air was fragrant with dewy scents, and the moon, already high above the tree-tops, poured down her gentle radiance upon the quaint, old garden with its winding walks, and clipped yew hedges, while upon the quiet, from the dim shadow of the distant woods, stole the soft, sweet song of a nightingale.

Bellew walked a path bordered with flowers, and checkered with silver patches of moon-light, drinking in the thousand beauties about him, staring up at the glory of the moon, the indigo of the sky, and listening to the voice of the lonely singer in the wood. And yet it was of none of these he was thinking as he paused under the shadow of "King Arthur,"—nor of Small Porges, nor of any one or anything in this world but only of the sudden, light touch of a warm, soft hand upon his. "Be that you, sir?" Bellew started and now he found that he had been sitting, all this while, with an empty pipe between his teeth, yet content therewith; wherefore he shook his head, and wondered.

"Be that you, Mr. Beloo, sir?"

"Yes Adam, it is I."

"Ah! an' how might you be feelin' now—arter your exercise wi' the pitch-fork, sir?"

"Very fit, I thank you, Adam. Sit down, and smoke, and let us converse together."

"Why thankee sir," answered Adam, producing the small, black clay pipe from his waistcoat pocket, and accepting Bellew's proffered pouch. "I've been up to the 'ouse a visitin' Prudence, the cook,—an' a rare cook she be, too, Mr. Beloo sir!"

"And a rare buxom girl into the bargain, Adam!"

"Oh, ah!—she's well enough, sir; I won't go for to deny as she's a fine, up-standing, well-shaped, tall, an' proper figure of a woman as ever was, sir,—though the Kentish lasses be a tidy lot, Mr. Beloo sir. But, Lord! when you come to think of her gift for Yorkshire Puddin', likewise jam-rollers, and seed-cake,—(which, though mentioned last, ain't by no manner o' means least),—when you come to think of her brew o' ale, an' cider, an' ginger wine,—why then—I'm took, sir, I'm took altogether, an' the 'Old Adam' inside o' me works hisself into such a state that if another chap—'specially that there Job Jagway gets lookin' her way too often, why it's got to get took out o' him, or took out o' me in good 'ard knocks, Mr. Belloo, sir."

"And when are you going to get married, Adam?"

"Well sir, we was thinkin' that if Miss Anthea has a good season, thisyear, we'd get it over an' done wi' some time in October, sir,—but it's all accordin'."

"According to what?"

"To the 'ops, sir,—the H-O-P-S—'ops, sir. They're comin' on fine,—ah! scrumptuous they be! If they don't take the blight, sir, they'll be the finest 'ops this side o' Maidstone. But then, if they do take the blight,—why then my 'opes is blighted likewise sir,—B-L-I-T-E-D,—blighted, Mr. Belloo sir!" which said, Adam laughed once, nodded his head several times, and relapsed into puffing silence.

"Mr. Cassilis was over to-day, Adam," said Bellew, after a while pursuing a train of thought.

"Ah sir!—I seen him,—'e also seen me. 'E told me as Job Jagway was up and about again,—likewise Job Jagway will be over 'ere to-morrow, along wi' the rest of 'em for the sale, sir."

"Ah yes,—the sale!" said Bellew, thoughtfully.

"To think o' that there Job Jagway a coming over here to buy Miss Anthea's furnitur' do set the Old Adam a workin' inside o' me to that amazin' extent as I can't sit still, Mr. Belloo sir! If that there Job crosses my path to-morrer—well—let 'im—look out, that's all!" saying which, Adam doubled up a huge, knotted fist and shook it at an imaginary Job.

"Adam," said Bellew, in the same thoughtful tone, "I wonder if you would do something for me?"

"Anything you ax me, sir, so long as you don't want me to—"

"I want you to buy some of that furniture for me."

"What!" exclaimed Adam, and vented his great laugh again, "well, if that ain't a good 'un, sir! why that's just w'ot I'm a going to do! Ye see, I ain't w'ot you might call a rich cove, nor yet a millionaire, but I've got a bit put by, an' I drawed out ten pound, yesterday. Thinks I,—'here's to save Miss Anthea's old sideboard, or the mirror as she's so fond of, or if not—why then a cheer or so,—they ain't a going to get it all,—not while I've got a pound or two,' I sez to myself."

"Adam," said Bellew, turning suddenly, "that sentiment does you credit, that sentiment makes me proud to have knocked you into a ditch,—shake hands, Adam." And there, beneath the great apple tree, while the moon looked on, they very solemnly shook hands.

"And now, Adam," pursued Bellew, "I want you to put back your ten pounds, keep it for Prudence,—because I happen to have rather more than we shall want,—see here!" And, with the words, Bellew took out a leathern wallet, and from this wallet, money, and bank-notes,—more money, and more bank-notes than Adam had ever beheld in all his thirty odd years, at sight of which his eyes opened, and his square jaw relaxed, to the imminent danger of his cherished clay pipe.

"I want you to take this," Bellew went on, counting a sum into Adam's nerveless hand, "and to-morrow, when the sale begins, if any one makes a bid for anything, I want you to bid higher, and, no matter what, you must always buy—always, you understand?"

"But sir,—that there old drorin'-room cab'net wi' the—carvings—"

"Buy it!"

"An' the silver candle-sticks,—and the four-post bed-stead,—an' the—"

"Buy 'em, Adam,—buy everything! If we haven't enough money there's plenty more where this came from,—only buy! —You understand?"

"Oh yes sir, I understand! 'Ow much 'ave you give me? Why, here's—forty-five,—fifty,—sixty,—Lord!—"

"Put it away, Adam,—forget all about it till to-morrow,—and not a word, mind!"

"A hundred pound!" gasped Adam, "Lord!—Oh I won't speak of it, trust me, Mr. Belloo, sir! But to think of me a walking about wi' a hundred pound in my pocket,—Lord! I won't say nothing—but to think of Old Adam wi' a hundred pound in his pocket, e'Cod! it do seem that comical!" saying which, Adam buttoned the money into a capacious pocket, slapped it, nodded, and rose. "Well sir, I'll be going,—there be Miss Anthea in the garden yonder, and if she was to see me now there's no sayin' but I should be took a laughin' to think o' this 'ere hundred pound."

"Miss Anthea!—where?"

"Comin' through the rose-gardin. She be off to see old Mother Dibbin. They call Mother Dibbin a witch, an' now as she's down wi' the rheumatics there ain't nobody to look arter 'er,—'cept Miss Anthea,—she'd ha' starved afore now if it 'adn't been for Miss Anthea, but Lord love your eyes, an' limbs, Mr. Belloo sir! Miss Anthea don't care if she's a witch, or fifty witches, not she! So good-night, Mr. Belloo sir, an' mum's the word!"

Saying which, Adam slapped his pocket again, nodded, winked, and went upon his way.

CHAPTER XI

Of the "Man with the Tiger Mark"

It is a moot question as to whether a curl can be more alluring when it glows beneath the fiery kisses of the sun, or shines demurely in the tender radiance of the moon. As Bellew looked at it now,—that same small curl that nodded and beckoned to him above Anthea's left ear,—he strongly inclined to the latter opinion.

"Adam tells me that you are going out, Miss Anthea."

"Only as far as Mrs. Dibbin's cottage,—just across the meadow."

"Adam also informs me that Mrs. Dibbin is a witch."

"People call her so."

"Never in all my days have I seen a genuine, old witch,—so I'll come with you, if I may?"

"Oh, this is a very gentle old witch, and she is neither humpbacked, nor does she ride a broom-stick,—so I'm afraid you'll be disappointed, Mr. Bellew."

"Then, at least, I can carry your basket,—allow me!" And so, in his quiet, masterful fashion he took the basket from her arm, and walked on beside her, through the orchard.

"What a glorious night it is!" exclaimed Anthea suddenly, drawing a deep breath of the fragrant air,—"Oh! it is good to be alive! In spite of all the cares, and worries, life is very sweet!"

After this, they walked on some distance in silence, she gazing wistfully upon the beauties of the familiar world about her while he watched the curl above her ear until she, becoming aware of it all at once, promptly sent it back into retirement, with a quick, deft little pat of her fingers.

"I hope," said Bellew at last, "I do sincerely hope that you 'tucked up' my nephew safe in bed,—you see—"

"Your nephew, indeed!"

"Our nephew, then; I ask because he tells me that he can't possibly sleep unless you go to 'tuck him up,'—and I can quite believe it."

"Do you know, Mr. Bellew, I'm growing quite jealous of you, he can't move a step without you, and he is for ever talking, and lauding your numberless virtues!"

"But then—I'm only an uncle, after all, and if he talks of me to you, he talks of you to me, all day long."

"Oh, does he!"

"And, among other things, he told me that I ought to see you when your hair is down, and all about you."

"Oh!" exclaimed Anthea.

"Indeed, our nephew is much luckier than I, because I never had an aunt of my own to come and 'tuck me up' at night with her hair hanging all about her—like a beautiful cloak. So, you see, I have no boyish recollections to go upon, but I think I can imagine—"

"And what do you think of the Sergeant?" Anthea enquired, changing the subject abruptly.

"I like him so much that I am going to take him at his word, and call upon him at the first opportunity."

"Did Aunt Priscilla tell you that he comes marching along regularly every day, at exactly the same hour?"

"Yes,—to see how the peaches are getting on!" nodded Bellew.

"For such a very brave soldier he is a dreadful coward," said Anthea, smiling, "it has taken him five years to screw up courage enough to tell her that she's uncommonly young for her age. And yet, I think it is just that diffidence that makes him so lovable. And he is so simple, and so gentle—in spite of all his war medals. When I am moody, and cross, the very sight of him is enough to put me in humour again."

"Has he never—spoken to Miss Priscilla,—?"

"Never,—though, of course, she knows, and has done from the very first. I asked him once, why he had never told her what it was brought him so regularly,—to look at the peaches, —and he said, in his quick, sharp way: 'Miss Anthea,—can't be done, mam,—a poor, battered, old soldier,—only one arm,—no mam.'"

"I wonder if one could find just such another Sergeant outside Arcadia," said Bellew, "I wonder!"

Now they were approaching a stile towards which Bellew had directed his eyes, from time to time, as, for that matter, curiously enough, had Anthea; but to him it seemed that it never would be reached, while to her, it seemed that it would be reached much too soon. Therefore she began to rack her mind trying to remember some gate, or any gap in the hedge that should obviate the necessity of climbing it. But, before she could recall any such gate, or gap, they were at the stile, and

Bellew, leaping over, had set down the basket, and stretched out his hand to aid her over. But Anthea, tall, and lithe, active and vigorous with her outdoor life, and used to such things from her infancy, stood a moment hesitating. To be sure, the stile was rather high, yet she could have vaulted it nearly, if not quite, as easily as Bellew himself, had she been alone. But then, she was not alone, moreover, be it remembered, this was in Arcadia of a mid-summer night. Thus, she hesitated, only a moment, it is true, for, seeing the quizzical look in his eyes that always made her vaguely rebellious,—with a quick, light movement, she mounted the stile, and there paused to shake her head in laughing disdain of his out-stretched hand; then— there was the sound of rending cambric, she tripped, and, next moment, he had caught her in his arms. It was for but a very brief instant that she lay, soft and yielding, in his embrace, yet she was conscious of how strong were the arms that held her so easily, ere they set her down.

"I beg your pardon!—how awkward I am!" she exclaimed, in hot mortification.

"No," said Bellew, shaking his head, "it was a nail, you know, a bent, and rusty nail,—here, under the top bar. Is your dress much torn?"

"Oh, that is nothing, thank you!"

So they went on again, but now they were silent once more, and very naturally, for Anthea was mightily angry,—with herself, the stile, Bellew, and everything concerned; while he was thinking of the sudden, warm clasp of her arms, of the alluring fragrance of her hair, and of the shy droop of her lashes as she lay in his embrace. Therefore, as he walked on beside her, saying nothing, within his secret soul he poured benedictions upon the head of that bent, and rusty nail.

And presently, having turned down a grassy lane and crossed a small but very noisy brook that chattered impertinences among the stones and chuckled at them slyly from the shadows, they eventually came upon a small, and very lonely little cottage bowered in roses and honeysuckle,—as are all the cottages hereabouts. But now Anthea paused, looking at Bellew with a dubious brow.

"I ought to warn you that Mrs. Dibbin is very old, and sometimes a little queer, and sometimes says very—surprising things."

"Excellent!" nodded Bellew, holding the little gate open for her, "very right and proper conduct in a witch, and I love surprises above all things."

But Anthea still hesitated, while Bellew stood with his hand upon the gate, waiting for her to enter. Now he had left his hat behind him, and, as the moon shone down on his bare head, she could not but notice how bright, and yellow was his hair, despite the thick, black brows below.

"I think I—would rather you waited outside,—if you don't mind, Mr. Bellew."

"You mean that I am to be denied the joy of conversing with a real, live, old witch, and having my fortune told?" he sighed. "Well, if such is your will—so be it," said he obediently, and handed her the basket.

"I won't keep you waiting very long,—and—thank you!" she smiled, and, hurrying up the narrow path, she tapped at the cottage door.

"Come in! come in!" cried an old, quavering voice, albeit, very sharp, and piercing. "That be my own soft dove of a maid,— my proud, beautiful, white lady! Come in! come in!—and bring him wi' you,—him as is so big, and strong,—him as I've expected so long,—the tall, golden man from over seas. Bid him come in, Miss Anthea, that Goody Dibbin's old eyes may look at him at last."

Hereupon, at a sign from Anthea, Bellew turned in at the gate, and striding up the path, entered the cottage.

Despite the season, a fire burned upon the hearth, and crouched over this, in a great elbow-chair, sat a very bent, and aged woman. Her face was furrowed, and seamed with numberless lines and wrinkles, but her eyes were still bright, and she wore no spectacles; likewise her white hair was wonderfully thick, and abundant, as could plainly be seen beneath the frill of her cap, for, like the very small room of this very small cottage, she was extremely neat, and tidy. She had a great, curving nose, and a great, curving chin, and what with this and her bright, black eyes, and stooping figure, she was very much like what a witch should be,—albeit a very superior kind of old witch.

She sat, for a while, staring up at Bellew who stood tall, and bare-headed, smiling down at her; and then, all at once, she nodded her head three several, and distinct times.

"Right!" she quavered, "right! right,—it be all right!—the golden man as I've watched this many an' many a day, wi' the curly hair, and the sleepy eye, and the Tiger-mark upon his arm,—right! right!"

"What do you mean by 'Tiger-mark?'" enquired Bellew.

"I mean, young master wi' your golden curls,—I mean as, sitting here day in, and day out, staring down into my fire, I has my dreams,—leastways, I calls 'em my dreams, though there's them as calls it the 'second sight.' But pray sit down, tall sir, on the stool there; and you, my tender maid, my dark lady, come you here—upon my right, and, if you wish, I'll look into the ink, or read your pretty hand, or tell you what I see down there in the fire. But no,—first, show what you have brought for Old Nannie in the blessed basket,—the fine, strong basket as holds so much. Yes, set it down here—where I can open it myself, tall sir. Eh,—what's this?—Tea! God bless you for the tea, my dear! And eggs, and butter,—and a cold chicken!—the Lord bless your kind heart, Miss Anthea! Ah, my proud lady, happy the man who shall win ye! Happy the man who shall wed ye, my dark, beautiful maid. And strong must he be, aye, and masterful he who shall wake the love-light in those dark, great, passionate eyes of yours. And there is no man in all this world can do it but he must be a golden man— wi' the Tiger-mark upon him."

"Why—oh Nannie—!"

"Aye,—blush if ye will, my dark lady, but Mother Dibbin knows she's seen it in the fire, dreamed it in her dreams, and read it in the ink. The path lies very dark afore ye, my lady,— aye very dark it be, and full o' cares, and troubles, but there's the sun shining beyond,—bright, and golden. You be proud, and high, and scornful, my lady,—'tis in your blood,—you'll need a strong hand to guide ye,—and the strong hand shall come. By force you shall be wooed, and by force you shall be wed,—and there be no man strong enough to woo, and wed ye, but him as I've told ye of—him as bears the Tiger-mark."

"But Nannie," said Anthea again, gently interrupting her, and patting the old woman's shrivelled hand, "you're forgetting the basket,—you haven't found all we've brought you, yet."

"Aye, aye!" nodded old Nannie, "the fine, strong basket,—let's see what more be in the good, kind basket. Here's bread, and sugar,—and—"

"A pound of your favourite tobacco!" said Anthea, with a smiling nod.

"Oh the good weed! The blessed weed!" cried the old woman, clutching the package with trembling fingers. "Ah! who can tell the comfort it has been to me in the long, long days, and the long, long nights,—the blessed weed! when I've sat here a looking and a looking into the fire. God bless you, my sweet maid, for your kindly thought!" and, with a sudden gesture, she caught Anthea's hand to her lips, and then, just as suddenly turned upon Bellew.

"And now, tall sir, can I do ought for ye? Shall I look into the fire for ye, or the ink, or read your hand?"

"Why yes," answered Bellew, stretching out his hand to her, "you shall tell me two things, if you will; first, shall one ever find his way into the 'Castle of Heart's Desire,' and secondly;—When?"

"Oh, but I don't need to look into your hand to tell you that, tall sir, nor yet in the ink, or in the fire, for I've dreamed it all in my dreams. And now, see you, 'tis a strong place, this Castle,—wi' thick doors, and great locks, and bars. But I have seen those doors broke' down,—those great locks, and bars burst asunder,—but—there is none can do this but him as bears the Tiger-Mark. So much for the first. And, for the second,—Happiness shall come a riding to you on the full moon,—but you must reach up—and take it for yourself,—if you be tall enough."

"And—even you are not tall enough to do that, Mr. Bellew!" laughed Anthea, as she rose to bid Old Nannie "Good-night," while Bellew, unnoticed, slipped certain coins upon a corner of the chimney-piece. So, old Nannie blessed them, and theirs, —past, present, and future, thoroughly and completely, with a fine comprehensiveness that only a genuinely accomplished old witch might hope to attain to, and, following them to the door, paused there with one shrivelled, claw-like hand up-lifted towards the sky:

"At the full o' the moon, tall sir!" she repeated, "at the full o' the moon! As for you, my dark-eyed lady, I say, by force you shall be wooed, and by force ye shall be wed, aye! aye!—but there is no man strong enough except he have the Tiger-Mark upon him. Old Nannie knows,—she's seen it in the ink, dreamed it in the fire, and read it all in your pretty hand. And now—thank ye for the tea, my pretty, and God bless ye for the good weed, and just so sure as you've been good, and kind to old Nannie, so shall Fortune be good and kind to you, Miss Anthea."

"Poor old Nannie!" said Anthea, as they went on down the grassy lane, "she is so very grateful for so little. And she is such a gentle old creature really, though the country folk do call her a witch and are afraid of her because they say she has the 'evil eye,'—which is ridiculous, of course! But nobody ever goes near her, and she is dreadfully lonely, poor old thing!"

"And so that is why you come to sit with her, and let her talk to you?" enquired Bellew, staring up at the moon.

"Yes."

"And do you believe in her dreams, and visions?"

"No,—of course not!" answered Anthea, rather hurriedly, and with a deeper colour in her cheeks, though Bellew was still intent upon the moon. "You don't either,—do you?" she enquired, seeing he was silent.

"Well, I don't quite know," he answered slowly, "but she is rather a wonderful old lady, I think."

"Yes, she has wonderful thick hair still," nodded Anthea, "and she's not a bit deaf, and her eyes are as clear, and sharp as ever they were."

"Yes, but I wasn't meaning her eyes, or her hair, or her hearing."

"Oh,—then pray what were you pleased to mean?"

"Did you happen to notice what she said about a—er—Man with, a—Tiger-Mark?" enquired Bellew, still gazing up at the moon.

Anthea laughed:

"The Man with the Tiger-Mark,—of course! he has been much in her dreams, lately, and she has talked of him a great deal,—"

"Has she?" said Bellew, "ha!"

"Yes,—her mind is full of strange twists, and fancies,—you see she is so very old,—and she loves to tell me her dreams, and read the future for me."

"Though, of course, you don't believe it," said Bellew.

"Believe it!" Anthea repeated, and walked some dozen paces, or so, before she answered,—"no, of course not."

"Then—none of your fortune,—nothing she told you has ever come true?"

Once more Anthea hesitated, this time so long that Bellew turned from his moon-gazing to look at her.

"I mean," he went on, "has none of it ever come true,—about this Man with the Tiger-Mark, for instance?"

"No,—oh no!" answered Anthea, rather hastily, and laughed again. "Old Nannie has seen him in her dreams—everywhere, —in India, and Africa, and China; in hot countries, and cold countries—oh! Nannie has seen him everywhere, but I have seen him—nowhere, and, of course, I never shall."

"Ah!" said Bellew, "and she reads him always in your fortune, does she?"

"And I listen very patiently," Anthea nodded, "because it pleases her so much, and it is all so very harmless, after all, isn't it?"

"Yes," answered Bellew, "and very wonderful!"

Jeffery Farnol

"Wonderful?—poor old Nannie's fancies!—What do you mean by wonderful?"

"Upon my word, I hardly know," said Bellew, shaking his head, "but 'there are more things in heaven, and earth,' etc., you know, and this is one of them."

"Really!—now you grow mysterious, Mr. Bellew."

"Like the night!" he answered, turning to aid her across the impertinent brook that chuckled at them, and laughed after them, as only such a very impertinent brook possibly could.

So, betimes, they reached the stile, and crossed it, this time without mishap, despite the lurking nail and, all too soon for Bellew, had traversed the orchard, and were come to the garden where the roses all hung so still upon their stems that they might have been asleep, and filling the air with the perfume of their dreams.

And here they paused, perhaps because of the witchery of the moon, perhaps to listen to the voice of the nightingale who sang on more gloriously than ever. Yet, though they stood so close together, their glances seldom met, and they were very silent. But at last, as though making up her mind, Anthea spoke:

"What did you mean when you said Old Nannie's dreams were so wonderful?" she asked.

"I'll show you!" he answered, and, while he spoke, slipped off his coat, and drawing up his shirt-sleeve, held out a muscular, white arm towards her. He held it out in the full radiance of the moon, and thus, looking down at it, her eyes grew suddenly wide, and her breath caught strangely as surprise gave place to something else; for there, plain to be seen upon the white flesh, were three long scars that wound up from elbow to shoulder. And so, for a while, they stood thus, she looking at his arm, and he at her.

"Why—" said she at last, finding voice in a little gasp,—"why then—"

"I am the Man with the Tiger Mark!" he said, smiling his slow, placid smile. Now, as his eyes looked down into hers, she flushed sudden, and hot, and her glance wavered, and fell beneath his.

"Oh!" she cried, and, with the word, turned about, and fled from him into the house.

CHAPTER XII

In which may be found a full, true, and particular account of the sale

"Uncle Porges, there's a little man in the hall with a red, red nose, an' a blue, blue chin,—"

"Yes, I've seen him,—also his nose, and chin, my Porges."

"But he's sticking little papers with numbers on them, all over my Auntie Anthea's chairs,—an' tables. Now what do you s'pose he's doing that for?"

"Who knows? It's probably all on account of his red nose, and blue chin, my Porges. Anyway, don't worry about him,—let us rather, find our Auntie Anthea."

They found her in the hall. And it *was* a hall, here, at Dapplemere, wide, and high, and with a minstrel's gallery at one end; a hall that, years and years ago, had often rung with the clash of men-at-arms, and echoed with loud, and jovial laughter, for this was the most ancient part of the Manor.

It looked rather bare, and barren, just now, for the furniture was all moved out of place,—ranged neatly round the walls, and stacked at the farther end, beneath the gallery where the little man in question, blue of chin, and red of nose, was hovering about it, dabbing little tickets on chairs, and tables, —even as Small Porges had said.

And, in the midst of it all, stood Anthea, a desolate figure, Bellew thought, who, upon his entrance, bent her head to draw on her driving gloves, for she was waiting for the dog-cart which was to bear her, and Small Porges to Cranbrook, far away from the hollow tap of the auctioneer's hammer.

"We're getting rid of some of the old furniture, you see, Mr. Bellew," she said, laying her hand on an antique cabinet nearby,—"we really have much more than we ever use."

"Yes," said Bellew. But he noticed that her eyes were very dark and wistful, despite her light tone, and that she had laid her hand upon the old cabinet with a touch very like a caress.

"Why is that man's nose so awful' red, and his chin so blue, Auntie Anthea?" enquired Small Porges, in a hissing stage whisper.

"Hush Georgy!—I don't know," said Anthea.

"An' why is he sticking his little numbers all over our best furniture!"

"That is to guide the auctioneer."

"Where to,—an' what is an auctioneer?"

But, at this moment, hearing the wheels of the dog-cart at the door, Anthea turned, and hastened out into the sunshine.

"A lovely day it do be for drivin'," said Adam touching his hat, "an' Bess be thinkin' the same, I do believe!" and he patted the glossy coat of the mare, who arched her neck, and pawed the gravel with an impatient hoof. Lightly, and nimbly Anthea swung herself up to the high seat, turning to make Small Porges secure beside her, as Bellew handed him up.

"You'll—look after things for me, Adam?" said Anthea, glancing back wistfully into the dim recesses of the cool, old hall.

"Aye,—I will that, Miss Anthea!"

"Mr. Bellew, we can find room for you if you care to come with us?"

"Thanks," said he, shaking his head, "but I rather think I'll stay here, and—er—help Adam to—to—look after things, if you don't mind."

"Then,—'Good-bye!'" said Anthea, and, nodding to Adam, he gave the mare her head, and off they went.

"Good-bye!" cried Small Porges, "an' thank you for the shilling Uncle Porges."

"The mare is—er—rather fresh this morning, isn't she, Adam?" enquired Bellew, watching the dog-cart's rapid course.

"Fresh sir?"

"And that's rather a—er—dangerous sort of thing for a woman to drive, isn't it?"

"Meanin' the dog-cart, sir?"

"Meaning the dog-cart, Adam."

"Why, Lord love ye, Mr. Belloo sir!" cried Adam with his great laugh, "there ain't nobody can 'andle the ribbons better than Miss Anthea,—there ain't a horse as she can't drive,—ah! or ride, for that matter,—not no-wheres, sir."

"Hum!" said Bellew, and, having watched the dog-cart out of sight, he turned and followed Adam into the stables.

And here, sitting upon a bale of hay, they smoked many pipes together in earnest converse, until such time as the sale should begin.

As the day advanced, people began arriving in twos and threes, and, among the first, the Auctioneer himself. A jovial-faced man, was this Auctioneer, with jovial manner, and a jovial smile. Indeed, his joviality seemed, somehow or other, to have got into the very buttons of his coat, for they fairly winked, and twinkled with joviality. Upon catching sight of the furniture he became, if possible, more jovial than ever, and beckoning to his assistant,—that is to say to the small man with the red nose and the blue chin, who, it seemed answered to the name of Theodore,—he clapped him jovially upon the back,—(rather as though he were knocking him down to some unfortunate bidder),—and immediately fell into business converse with him,—albeit jovial still.

But all the while intending purchasers were arriving; they came on horse, and afoot, and in conveyances of every sort and kind, and the tread of their feet, and the buzz of their voices awoke unwonted echoes in the old place. And still they came, from far and near, until some hundred odd people were crowded into the hall.

Conspicuous among them was a large man with a fat, red neck which he was continually mopping at, and rubbing with a vivid bandanna handkerchief scarcely less red. Indeed, red seemed to be his pervading colour, for his hair was red, his hands were red, and his face, heavy and round, was reddest of all, out of whose flaming circumference two diminutive but very sharp eyes winked and blinked continually. His voice, like himself, was large with a peculiar brassy ring to it that penetrated to the farthest corners and recesses of the old hall. He was, beyond all doubt, a man of substance, and of no small importance, for he was greeted deferentially on all hands, and it was to be noticed that people elbowed each other to make way for him, as people ever will before substance, and property. To some of them he nodded, to some he spoke, and with others he even laughed, albeit he was of a solemn, sober, and serious nature, as becomes a man of property, and substance.

Between whiles, however, he bestowed his undivided attention upon the furniture. He sat down suddenly and heavily, in chairs; he pummelled them with his plump, red fists, —whereby to test their springs; he opened the doors of cabinets; he peered into drawers; he rapped upon tables, and altogether comported himself as a thoroughly knowing man should, who is not to be hocussed by veneer, or taken in by the shine, and splendour of well applied bees-wax. Bellew, watching all this from where he sat screened from the throng by a great carved sideboard, and divers chairs, and whatnots, —drew rather harder at his pipe, and, chancing to catch Adam's eye, beckoned him to approach.

"Who is that round, red man, yonder, Adam?" he enquired, nodding to where the individual in question was engaged at that moment poking at something or other with a large, sausage-like finger.

"That!" replied Adam in a tone of profound disgust, "that be Mr. Grimes, o' Cranbrook, sir. Calls hisself a corn-chandler, —but I calls 'im,—well, never mind what, sir,—only it weren't at corn-chandling as 'e made all 'is money, sir,—and it be him as we all work, and slave for,—here at Dapplemere Farm."

"What do you mean, Adam?"

"I mean as it be him as holds the mortgage on Dapplemere, sir."

"Ah,—and how much?"

"Over three thousand pound, Mr. Belloo sir!" sighed Adam, with a hopeless shake of the head, "an' that be a powerful lot o' money, sir."

Bellew thought of the sums he had lavished upon his yacht, upon his three racing cars, and certain other extravagances. Three thousand pounds,—fifteen thousand dollars! It would make her a free woman,—independent,—happy! Just fifteen thousand dollars,—and he had thrown away more than that upon a poker game, before now!

"Lord!" exclaimed Adam, "the very sight o' that theer Grimes's pig eyes a-starin' at Miss Anthea's furnitur' do make the Old Adam rise up in me to that amazin' extent, Mr. Belloo sir —why, jest look at 'im a-thumpin' an' a poundin' at that theer chair!" Saying which, Adam turned, and elbowing his way to where Mr. Grimes was in the act of testing the springs of an easy chair, he promptly,—and as though forced by a struggling mob,—fell up against Mr. Grimes, and jostled Mr. Grimes, and trod heavily upon the toes of Mr. Grimes, and all with an expression of the most profound unconsciousness and abstraction, which, upon the indignant Corn-chandler's loud expostulations, immediately changed to a look of innocent surprise.

"Can't you look where you're going?—you clumsy fool!" fumed the irate Grimes, redder of neck than ever.

"Ax your pardon, Mr. Grimes," said Adam solemnly, "but what wi' people's legs, an' cheer legs, an' the legs o' tables, —not to mention sideboards an' cab'nets,—which, though not 'aving no legs, ain't to be by no manner o' means despised therefore,—w'ot wi' this an' that, an' t'other, I am that con- fined, or as you might say, con-fused, I don't know which legs is mine, or yourn, or anybody else's. Mr. Grimes sir,—I makes so bold as to ax your pardon all over again, sir." During which speech, Adam contrived, once more, to fall against, to tread upon, and to jostle the highly incensed Mr. Grimes back into the crowd again. Thereafter he became a Nemesis to Mr. Grimes, haunting him through the jungle of chairs, and tables, pursuing him into distant corners, and shady places, where, so sure as the sausage-like finger poised itself for an interrogatory poke, or the fat, red fist doubled itself for a spring-testing punch, the innocent-seeming Adam would thereupon fall against him from the rear, sideways, or in front.

Meanwhile, Bellew sat in his secluded corner, watching the

crowd through the blue wreaths of his pipe, but thinking of her who, brave though she was, had nevertheless run away from it all at the last moment. Presently, however, he was aware that the Corn-chandler had seated himself on the other side of the chiffonier, puffing, and panting with heat, and indignation,—where he was presently joined by another individual,—a small, rat-eyed man, who bid Mr. Grimes a deferential "Good-day!"

"That there Adam," puffed the Corn-chandler, "that there Adam ought to be throwed out into the stables where he belongs. I never see a man as was so much growed to feet and elbers, in all my days! He ought to be took," repeated the Corn-chandler, "and shook, and throwed out into the yard."

"Yes," nodded the other, "took, and shook, and throwed out— neck, and crop, sir! And now,—what might you think o' the furniture, Mr. Grimes?"

"So so, Parsons," nodded Grimes, "so so!"

"Shall you buy?"

"I am a-going," said the Corn-chandler with much delibe-ration, "I am a-going to take them tapestry cheers, sir, likewise the grand-feyther clock in the corner here, likewise the four-post bed-stead wi' the carved 'ead-board,—and—most particular, Parsons, I shall take this here side-board. There ain't another piece like this in the county, as I know of,—solid ma-hogany, sir!—and the carvings!" and herewith, he gave two loud double knocks upon the article of furniture in question. "Oh! I've 'ad my eye on this side-board for years, and years, —knowed I'd get it some day, too,—the only wonder is as she ain't had to sell up afore now."

"Meaning Miss Anthea, sir?"

"Ah,—her! I say as it's a wonder to me,—wo't wi' the interest on the mortgage I 'old on the place, and one thing and another,—it's a wonder to me as she's kept her 'ead above water so long. But—mark me, Parsons, mark me,—she'll be selling again soon, and next time it'll be lock, stock, and barrel, Parsons!"

"Well, I don't 'old wi' women farmers, myself!" nodded Parsons. "But,—as to that cup-board over there,—Sheraton, I think,—what might you suppose it to be worth,—betwixt friends, now?" enquired Parsons, the rat eyed.

"Can't say till I've seed it, and likewise felt it," answered the Corn-chandler, rising. "Let me lay my 'and upon it, and I'll tell you—to a shilling," and here, they elbowed their way into the crowd. But Bellew sat there, chin in hand, quite oblivious to the fact that his pipe was out, long since.

The tall, old grand-father clock ticking in leisurely fashion in the corner behind him, solemn and sedate, as it had done since, (as the neat inscription upon the dial testified), it had first been made in the Year of Grace 1732, by one Jabez Havesham, of London;—this ancient time-piece now uttered a sudden wheeze, (which, considering its great age, could scarcely be wondered at), and, thereafter, the wheezing having subsided, gave forth a soft, and mellow chime, proclaiming to all and sundry, that it was twelve o'clock. Hereupon, the Auctioneer, bustling to and fro with his hat upon the back of his head, consulted his watch, nodded to the red nosed, blue-chinned Theodore, and, perching himself above the crowd, gave three sharp knocks with his hammer.

"Gentlemen!" he began, but here he was interrupted by a loud voice upraised in hot anger.

"Confound ye for a clumsy rascal! Will ye keep them elbers o' yourn to out o' my weskit, eh? Will ye keep them big feet o' yourn to yeself? If there ain't room enough for ye,—out ye go, d'ye hear—I'll have ye took, and shook,—and throwed out where ye belong; so jest mind where ye come a trampin', and a treadin'."

"Tread!" repeated Adam, "Lord! where am I to tread? If I steps backward I tread on ye,—If I steps sideways I tread on ye, if I steps for-ard I tread on ye. It do seem to me as I can't go nowhere but there you be a-waitin' to be trod on, Mr. Grimes, sir."

Hereupon the Auctioneer rapped louder than ever, upon which, the clamour subsiding, he smiled his most jovial smile, and once more began:

"Gentlemen! you have all had an opportunity to examine the furniture I am about to dispose of, and, as fair minded human beings I think you will admit that a finer lot of genuine antique was never offered at one and the same time. Gentlemen, I am not going to burst forth into laudatory rodomontade, (which is a word, gentlemen that I employ only among an enlightened community such as I now have the honour of addressing),—neither do I propose to waste your time in purposeless verbiage, (which is another of the same kind, gentlemen),—therefore, without further preface, or preamble, we will proceed at once to business. The first lot I have to offer you is a screen,—six foot high,—bring out the screen, Theodore! There it is, gentlemen,—open it out, Theodore! Observe, Gentlemen it is carved rosewood, the panels hand painted, and representing shepherds, and shepherdesses, disporting themselves under a tree with banjo and guitar. Now what am I offered for this hand-painted, antique screen,—come?"

"Fifteen shillings!" from someone deep hidden in the crowd.

"Start as low as you like, gentlemen! I am offered a miserable fifteen shillings for a genuine, hand-painted—"

"Sixteen!" this from a long, loose-limbed fellow with a patch over one eye, and another on his cheek.

"A pound!" said Adam, promptly.

"A guinea!" nodded he of the patches.

"Twenty-five shillin's!" said Adam.

"At twenty-five shillings!" cried the Auctioneer, "any advance? —a genuine, hand-painted, antique screen,—going at twenty-five—at twenty-five,—going—going—gone! To the large gentleman in the neckcloth, Theodore!"

"Theer be that Job Jagway, sir," said Adam, leaning across the side-board to impart this information,—"over yonder, Mr. Belloo sir,—'im as was bidding for the screen,—the tall chap wi' the patches. Two patches be pretty good, but I do wish as I'd give him a couple more, while I was about it, Mr. Belloo sir." Here, the Auctioneer's voice put an end to Adam's self-reproaches, and he turned back to the business in hand.

"The next lot I'm going to dispose of, gentlemen, is a fine set of six chairs with carved antique backs, and upholstered in tapestry. Also two arm-chairs to match,—wheel 'em out, Theodore! Now what is your price for these eight fine pieces,—look 'em over and bid accordingly."

"Thirty shillings!" Again from the depths of the crowd.

"Ha! ha!—you joke sir!" laughed the Auctioneer, rubbing his hands in his most jovial manner, "you joke! I can't see you, but you joke of course, and I laugh accordingly, ha! ha! Thirty shillings for eight, fine, antique, tapestried, hand-carved chairs,—Oh very good,—excellent, upon my soul!"

"Three pound!" said the fiery-necked Corn-chandler.

"Guineas!" said the rat-eyed Parsons.

"Four pound!" nodded the Corn-chandler.

"Four pound ten!" roared Adam.

"Five!" nodded Grimes, edging away from Adam's elbow.

"Six pound ten!" cried Adam.

"Seven!"—from Parsons.

"Eight!" said Grimes.

"Ten!" roared Adam, growing desperate.

"Eleven!" said Grimes, beginning to mop at his neck again.

Adam hesitated; eleven pounds seemed so very much for those chairs, that he had seen Prudence and the rosy-cheeked maids dust regularly every morning, and then,—it was not his money, after all. Therefore Adam hesitated, and glanced wistfully towards a certain distant corner.

"At eleven,—at eleven pounds!—this fine suite of hand-carved antique chairs, at eleven pounds!—at eleven!—at eleven, going —going!—"

"Fifteen!" said a voice from the distant corner; whereupon Adam drew a great sigh of relief, while the Corn-chandler contorted himself in his efforts to glare at Bellew round the side-board.

"Fifteen pounds!" chanted the Auctioneer, "I have fifteen,—I am given fifteen,—any advance? These eight antique chairs, going at fifteen!—going! for the last time,—going!—gone! Sold to the gentleman in the corner behind the side-board, Theodore."

"They were certainly fine chairs, Mr. Grimes!" said Parsons shaking his head.

"So so!" said the Corn-chandler, sitting down heavily, "So so, Parsons!" and he turned to glare at Bellew, who, lying back in an easy chair with his legs upon another, puffed at his pipe, and regarded all things with a placid interest.

It is not intended to record in these pages all the bids that were made as the afternoon advanced, for that would be fatiguing to write, and a weariness to read; suffice it that lots were put up, and regularly knocked down but always to Bellew, or Adam. Which last, encouraged by Bellew's bold advances, gaily roared down, and constantly out-bid all competitors with such unhesitating pertinacity, that murmurs rose, and swelled into open complaint. In the midst of which, the fiery-visaged Corn-chandler, purple now, between heat, and vexation, loudly demanded that he lay down some substantial deposit upon what he had already purchased, failing which, he should, there and then, be took, and shook, and throwed out into the yard.

"Neck, and crop!" added Mr. Parsons.

"That seems to be a fair proposition," smiled the Auctioneer, who had already experienced some doubts as to Adam's financial capabilities, yet with his joviality all unruffled,—"that seems to be a very fair proposal indeed. If the gentleman will put down some substantial deposit now—"

"Aye, for sure!" nodded Adam, stepping forward; and, unbuttoning a capacious pocket he drew out a handful of bank-notes, "shall I gi'e ye a hundred pound,—or will fifty be enough?"

"Why," said the Auctioneer, rubbing his hands as he eyed the fistful of bank-notes, "ten pound will be all that is necessary, sir,—just to ensure good faith, you understand."

Hereupon, Bellew beckoning to Adam, handed him a like amount which was duly deposited with the Auctioneer.

So, once more, the bidding began,—once more lots were put up,—and knocked down—now to Adam, and now to Bellew. The bed with the carved head-board had fallen to Adam after a lively contest between him, and Parsons, and the

Corn-chandler, which had left the latter in a state of perspiring profanity, from which he was by no means recovered, when the Auctioneer once more rapped for silence.

"And now, gentlemen, last, but by no means least, we come to the gem of the sale,—a side-board, gentlemen,—a magnificent, mahogany side-board, being a superb example of the carver's art! Here is a side-board, gentlemen, which,—if it can be equalled,—cannot be excelled—no, gentlemen, not if you were to search all the baronial halls, and lordly mansions in this land of mansions, and baronials. It is a truly magnificent piece, in perfect condition,—and to be sold at your own price. I say no more. Gentlemen,—how much for this magnificent, mahogany piece?"

"Ten pound!"

"Eleven!"

"Fifteen!"

"Seventeen!" said Adam, who was rapidly drawing near the end of his resources.

"Eighteen!" This from Job Jagway.

"Go easy there, Job!" hissed Adam, edging a little nearer to him, "go easy, now,—Nineteen!"

"Come, come Gentlemen!" remonstrated the Auctioneer, "this isn't a coal-scuttle, nor a broom, nor yet a pair of tongs,—this is a magnificent mahogany side-board,—and you offer me— nineteen pound!"

"Twenty!" said Job.

"Twenty-one!" roared Adam, making his last bid, and then, turning, he hissed in Job's unwilling ear,—"go any higher, an' I'll pound ye to a jelly, Job!"

"Twenty-five!" said Parsons.

"Twenty-seven!"

"Twenty-eight!"

"Thirty!" nodded Grimes, scowling at Adam.

"Thirty-two!" cried Parsons.

"Thirty-six!"

"Thirty-seven!"

"Forty!" nodded Grimes.

"That drops me," said Parsons, sighing, and shaking his head.

"Ah!" chuckled the Corn-chandler, "well, I've waited years for that side-board, Parsons, and I ain't going to let you take it away from me—nor nobody else, sir!"

"At forty!" cried the Auctioneer, "at forty!—this magnifi—"

"One!" nodded Bellew, beginning to fill his pipe.

"Forty-one's the bid,—I have forty-one from the gent in the corner—"

"Forty-five!" growled the Corn-chandler.

"Six!" said Bellew.

"Fifty!" snarled Grimes.

"One!" said Bellew.

"Gent in the corner gives me fifty-one!" chanted the Auctioneer—"any advance?—at fifty-one—"

"Fifty-five!" said Grimes, beginning to mop at his neck harder than ever.

"Add ten!" nodded Bellew.

"What's that?" cried Grimes, wheeling about.

"Gent in the corner offers me sixty-five,—at sixty-five,—this magnificent piece at sixty-five! What, are you all done?—at sixty-five, and cheap at the price,—come, gentlemen, take your time, give it another look over, and bid accordingly."

The crowd had dwindled rapidly during the last hour, which was scarcely to be wondered at seeing that they were constantly out-bid—either by a hoarse voiced, square-shouldered fellow in a neck-cloth, or a dreamy individual who lolled in a corner, and puffed at a pipe.

But now, as Grimes, his red cheeks puffed out, his little eyes snapping in a way that many knew meant danger (with a large D)—as the rich Corn-chandler, whose word was law to a good many, turned and confronted this lounging, long-legged individual,—such as remained closed round them in a ring, in keen expectation of what was to follow. Observing which, the Corn-chandler feeling it incumbent upon him now or never, to vindicate himself as a man of property, and substance, and not to be put down, thrust his hands deep into his pockets, spread his legs wide apart, and stared at Bellew in a way that most people had found highly disconcerting, before now. Bellew, however, seemed wholly unaffected, and went on imperturbably filling his pipe.

"At sixty-five!" cried the Auctioneer, leaning towards Grimes with his hammer poised, "at sixty-five—Will you make it another pound, sir!—come,—what do you say?"

"I say—no sir!" returned the Corn-chandler, slowly, and impressively, "I say no, sir,—I say—make it another—twenty pound, sir!" Hereupon heads were shaken, or nodded, and there rose the sudden shuffle of feet as the crowd closed in nearer.

"I get eighty-five! any advance on eighty-five?"

"Eighty-six!" said Bellew, settling the tobacco in his pipe-bowl with his thumb.

Once again the Auctioneer leaned over and appealed to the Corn-chandler, who stood in the same attitude, jingling the money in his pocket, "Come sir, don't let a pound or so stand between you and a side-board that can't be matched in the length and breadth of the United Kingdom,—come, what do you say to another ten shillings?"

"I say, sir," said Grimes, with his gaze still riveted upon Bellew, "I say—no sir,—I say make it another—twenty pound sir!"

Again there rose the shuffle of feet, again heads were nodded, and elbows nudged neighbouring ribs, and all eyes were focussed upon Bellew who was in the act of lighting his pipe.

"One hundred and six pounds!" cried the Auctioneer, "at one six!—at one six!—"

Bellew struck a match, but the wind from the open casement behind him, extinguished it.

"I have one hundred and six pounds! is there any advance, yes or no?—going at one hundred and six!"

Adam who, up till now, had enjoyed the struggle to the utmost, experienced a sudden qualm of fear.

Bellew struck another match.

"At one hundred and six pounds!—at one six,—going at one hundred and six pounds—!"

A cold moisture started out on Adam's brow, he clenched his hands, and muttered between his teeth. Supposing the money were all gone, like his own share, supposing they had to lose this famous old side-board,—and to Grimes of all people! This, and much more, was in Adam's mind while the Auctioneer held his hammer poised, and Bellew went on lighting his pipe.

"Going at one hundred and six!—going!—going!—"

"Fifty up!" said Bellew. His pipe was well alight at last, and he was nodding to the Auctioneer through a fragrant cloud.

"What!" cried Grimes, "ow much?"

"Gent in the corner gives me one hundred and fifty six pounds," said the Auctioneer, with a jovial eye upon the Corn-chandler's lowering visage, "one five six,—all done?—any advance? Going at one five six,—going! going!—gone!" The hammer fell, and with its tap a sudden silence came upon the old hall. Then, all at once, the Corn-chandler turned, caught up his hat, clapped it on, shook a fat fist at Bellew, and crossing to the door, lumbered away, muttering maledictions as he went.

By twos and threes the others followed him until there remained only Adam, Bellew, the Auctioneer, and the red-nosed Theodore. And yet, there was one other, for, chancing to raise his eyes to the minstrel's gallery, Bellew espied Miss Priscilla, who, meeting his smiling glance, leaned down suddenly over the carved rail, and very deliberately, threw him a kiss, and then hurried away with a quick, light tap-tap of her stick.

CHAPTER XIII

How Anthea came home

"Lord!" said Adam, pausing with a chair under either arm, "Lord, Mr. Belloo sir,—I wonder what Miss Anthea will say?" with which remark he strode off with the two chairs to set them in their accustomed places.

Seldom indeed had the old hall despite its many years, seen such a running to and fro, heard such a patter of flying feet, such merry voices, such gay, and heart-felt laughter. For here was Miss Priscilla, looking smaller than ever, in a great arm chair whence she directed the disposal and arrangement of all things, with quick little motions of her crutch-stick. And here were the two rosy-cheeked maids, brighter and rosier than ever, and here was comely Prudence hither come from her kitchen to bear a hand, and here, as has been said, was Adam, and here also was Bellew, his pipe laid aside with his coat, pushing, and tugging in his efforts to get the great side-board back into its customary position; and all, as has also been said, was laughter, and bustle, and an eager haste to have all things as they were,—and should be henceforth,—before Anthea's return.

"Lord!" exclaimed Adam again, balanced now upon a ladder, and pausing to wipe his brow with one hand and with a picture swinging in the other, "Lord! what ever will Miss Anthea say, Mr. Belloo sir!"

Jeffery Farnol

"Ah!" nodded Bellew thoughtfully, "I wonder!"

"What do you suppose she'll say, Miss Priscilla, mam?"

"I think you'd better be careful of that picture, Adam!"

"Which means," said Bellew, smiling down into Miss Priscilla's young, bright eyes, "that you don't know."

"Well, Mr. Bellew, she'll be very—glad, of course,—happier I think, than you or I can guess, because I know she loves every stick, and stave of that old furniture,—but—"

"But!" nodded Bellew, "yes, I understand."

"Mr. Bellew, if Anthea,—God bless her dear heart!—but if she has a fault—it is pride, Mr. Bellew, Pride! Pride! Pride!—with a capital P!"

"Yes, she is very proud."

"She'll be that 'appy-'earted," said Adam, pausing near-by with a great armful of miscellaneous articles, "an' that full o' joy as never was! Mr. Belloo sir!" Having delivered himself of which, he departed with his load.

"I rose this morning—very early, Mr. Bellew,—Oh! very early!" said Miss Priscilla, following Adam's laden figure with watchful eyes, "couldn't possibly sleep, you see. So I got up, —ridiculously early,—but, bless you, she was before me!"

"Ah!"

"Oh dear yes!—had been up—hours! And what—what do you suppose she was doing?" Bellew shook his head.

"She was rubbing and polishing that old side-board that you paid such a dreadful price for,—down on her knees before it,—yes she was! And polishing, and rubbing, and—crying all the while. Oh dear heart! Such great, big tears,—and so very quiet! When she heard my little stick come tapping along she tried to hide them,—I mean her tears, of course, Mr. Bellew, and when I drew her dear, beautiful head down into my arms, she—tried to smile. 'I'm so very silly, Aunt Priscilla,' she said, crying more than ever, 'but it *is* so hard to let the old things be taken away,—you see,—I do *love* them so! I tell you all this, Mr. Bellew, because I like you,—ever since you took the trouble to pick up a ball of worsted for a poor, old lame woman—in an orchard,—first impressions, you know. And secondly, I tell you all this to explain to you why I—hum!—"

"Threw a kiss—from a minstrel's gallery, to a most unworthy individual, Aunt Priscilla?"

"Threw you a kiss, Mr. Bellew,—I had to,—the side-board you know,—on her knees—you understand?"

"I understand!"

"You see, Mr. Belloo sir," said Adam, at this juncture, speaking from beneath an inlaid table which he held balanced upon his head,—"it ain't as if this was jest ordinary furnitur' sir,—ye see she kind-er feels as it be all part o' Dapplemere Manor, as it used to be called, it's all been here so long, that them cheers an' tables has come to be part o' the 'ouse, sir. So when she comes, an' finds as it ain't all been took,—or, as you might say,—vanished away,—why the question as I ax's you is, —w'ot will she say? Oh Lord!" And here, Adam gave vent to his great laugh which necessitated an almost superhuman exertion of strength to keep the table from slipping from its precarious perch. Whereupon Miss Priscilla screamed, (a very small scream, like herself) and Prudence scolded, and the two rosy-cheeked maids tittered, and Adam went chuckling upon his way.

And when the hall was, once more, its old, familiar, comfortable self, when the floor had been swept of its litter, and every trace of the sale removed,—then Miss Priscilla sighed, and

Bellew put on his coat.

"When do you expect—she will come home?" he enquired, glancing at the grandfather clock in the corner.

"Well, if she drove straight back from Cranbrook she would be here now,—but I fancy she won't be so very anxious to get home to-day,—and may come the longest way round; yes, it's in my mind she will keep away from Dapplemere as long as ever she can."

"And I think," said Bellew, "Yes, I think I'll take a walk. I'll go and call upon the Sergeant."

"The Sergeant!" said Miss Priscilla, "let me see,—it is now a quarter to six, it should take you about fifteen minutes to the village, that will make it exactly six o'clock. You will find the Sergeant just sitting down in the chair on the left hand side of the fire-place,—in the corner,—at the 'King's Head,' you know. Not that I have ever seen him there,—good gracious no! but I—happen to be—acquainted with his habits, and he is as regular and precise as his great, big silver watch, and that is the most precise, and regular thing in all the world. I am glad you are going," she went on, "because to-day is—well, a day apart, Mr. Bellew. You will find the Sergeant at the 'King's Head,' —until half past seven."

"Then I will go to the 'King's Head,'" said Bellew. "And what message do you send him?"

"None," said Miss Priscilla, laughing and shaking her head, —"at least,—you can tell him, if you wish,—that—the peaches are riper than ever they were this evening."

"I won't forget," said Bellew, smiling, and went out into the sunshine. But, crossing the yard, he was met by Adam, who, chuckling still, paused to touch his hat.

"To look at that theer 'all, sir, you wouldn't never know as there'd ever been any sale at all,—not no'ow. Now the only question as worrits me, and as I'm a-axin' of myself constant is,—what will Miss Anthea 'ave to say about it?"

"Yes," said Bellew, "I wonder!" And so he turned, and went away slowly across the fields.

Miss Priscilla had been right,—Anthea *was* coming back the longest way round,—also she was anxious to keep away from Dapplemere as long as possible. Therefore, despite Small Porges' exhortations, and Bess's champing impatience, she held the mare in, permitting her only the slowest of paces, which was a most unusual thing for Anthea to do. For the most part, too, she drove in silence seemingly deaf to Small Porges' flow of talk, which was also very unlike in her. But before her eyes were visions of her dismantled home, in her ears was the roar of voices clamouring for her cherished possessions,—a sickening roar, broken, now and then, by the hollow tap of the auctioneer's cruel hammer. And, each time the clamouring voices rose, she shivered, and every blow of the cruel hammer seemed to fall upon her quivering heart. Thus, she was unwontedly deaf and unresponsive to Small Porges, who presently fell into a profound gloom, in consequence; and thus, she held in the eager mare who therefore, shied, and fidgeted, and tossed her head indignantly.

But, slowly as they went, they came within sight of the house, at last, with its quaint gables, and many latticed windows, and the blue smoke curling up from its twisted chimneys,—smiling and placid as though, in all this great world, there were no such thing to be found as—an auctioneer's hammer.

And presently they swung into the drive, and drew up in the courtyard. And there was Adam, waiting to take the mare's head,—Adam, as good-natured, and stolid as though there were no abominations called, for want of a worse name, —sales.

Very slowly, for her, Anthea climbed down from the high

dog-cart, aiding Small Porges to earth, and with his hand clasped tight in hers, and with lips set firm, she turned and entered the hall. But, upon the threshold, she stopped, and stood there utterly still, gazing, and gazing upon the trim orderliness of everything. Then, seeing every well remembered thing in its appointed place,—all became suddenly blurred, and dim, and, snatching her hand from Small Porges' clasp, she uttered a great, choking sob, and covered her face.

But Small Porges had seen, and stood aghast, and Miss Priscilla had seen, and now hurried forward with a quick tap, tap of her stick. As she came, Anthea raised her head, and looked for one who should have been there, but was not. And, in that moment, instinctively she knew how things came to be as they were,—and, because of this knowledge, her cheeks flamed with a swift, burning colour, and with a soft cry, she hid her face in Miss Priscilla's gentle bosom. Then, while her face was yet hidden there, she whispered:

"Tell me—tell me—all about it."

But, meanwhile, Bellew, striding far away across the meadows, seeming to watch the glory of the sun-set, and to hearken to a blackbird piping from the dim seclusion of the copse a melodious "Good-bye" to the dying day, yet saw, and heard it not at all, for his mind was still occupied with Adam's question:—

"What would Miss Anthea say?"

CHAPTER XIV

Which, among, other things, has to do with shrimps, muffins,
and tin whistles

A typical Kentish Village is Dapplemere with its rows of scattered cottages bowered in roses and honeysuckle,—white walled cottages with steep-pitched roofs, and small latticed windows that seem to stare at all and sundry like so many winking eyes.

There is an air redolent of ripening fruit, and hops, for Dapplemere is a place of orchards, and hop-gardens, and rickyards, while, here and there, the sharp-pointed, red-tiled roof of some oast-house pierces the green.

Though Dapplemere village is but a very small place indeed, now-a-days,—yet it possesses a church, grey and ancient, whose massive Norman tower looks down upon gable and chimney, upon roof of thatch and roof of tile, like some benignant giant keeping watch above them all. Near-by, of course, is the inn, a great, rambling, comfortable place, with time-worn settles beside the door, and with a mighty sign a-swinging before it, upon which, plainly to be seen (when the sun catches it fairly) is that which purports to be a likeness of His Majesty King William the Fourth, of glorious memory. But alas! the colours have long since faded, so that now, (upon a dull day), it is a moot question whether His Majesty's nose was of the Greek, or Roman order, or, indeed, whether he was blessed with any nose at all. Thus, Time and Circumstances

have united to make a ghost of the likeness (as they have done
of the original, long since) which, fading yet more, and more,
will doubtless eventually vanish altogether,—like King William
himself, and leave but a vague memory behind.

Now, before the inn was a small crowd gathered about a trap
in which sat two men, one of whom Bellew recognised as the
rednecked Corn-chandler Grimes, and the other, the rat-eyed
Parsons.

The Corn-chandler was mopping violently at his face and neck
down which ran, and to which clung, a foamy substance
suspiciously like the froth of beer, and, as he mopped, his loud
brassy voice shook and quavered with passion.

"I tell ye—you shall get out o' my cottage!" he was saying, "I
say you shall quit my cottage at the end o' the month,—and
when I says a thing, I means it,—I say you shall get off of my
property,—you—and that beggarly cobbler. I say you shall be
throwed out o' my cottage,—lock, stock, and barrel. I say—"

"I wouldn't, Mr. Grimes,—leastways, not if I was you,"
another voice broke in, calm and deliberate. "No, I wouldn't
go for to say another word, sir; because, if ye do say another
word, I know a man as will drag you down out o' that cart,
sir,—I know a man as will break your whip over your very own
back, sir,—I know a man as will then take and heave you into
the horse-pond, sir,—and that man is me—Sergeant Appleby,
late of the Nineteenth Hussars, sir."

The Corn-chandler having removed most of the froth from his
head and face, stared down at the straight, alert figure of the
big Sergeant, hesitated, glanced at the Sergeant's fist which,
though solitary, was large, and powerful, scowled at the
Sergeant from his polished boots to the crown of his well-
brushed hat (which perched upon his close-cropped, grey hair
at a ridiculous angle totally impossible to any but an ex-
cavalry-man), muttered a furious oath, and snatching his whip,
cut viciously at his horse, very much as if that animal had been

the Sergeant himself, and, as the trap lurched forward, he shook his fist, and nodded his head.

"Out ye go,—at the end o' the month,—mind that!" he snarled and so, rattled away down the road still mopping at his head and neck until he had fairly mopped himself out of sight.

"Well, Sergeant," said Bellew extending his hand, "how are you!"

"Hearty, sir,—hearty I thank you, though, at this precise moment, just a leetle put out, sir. None the less I know a man as is happy to see you, Mr. Bellew, sir,—and that's me—Sergeant Appleby, at your service, sir. My cottage lies down the road yonder, an easy march—if you will step that far?—Speaking for my comrade and myself—we shall be proud for you to take tea with us—muffins sir—shrimps, Mr. Bellew—also a pikelet or two.—Not a great feast—but tolerable good rations, sir—and plenty of 'em—what do you say?"

"I say—done, and thank you very much!"

So, without further parley, the Sergeant saluted divers of the little crowd, and, wheeling sharply, strode along beside Bellew, rather more stiff in the back, and fixed of eye than was his wont, and jingling his imaginary spurs rather more loudly than usual.

"You will be wondering at the tantrums of the man Grimes, sir,—of his ordering me and my comrade Peterday out of his cottage. Sir—I'll tell you—in two words. It's all owing to the sale—up at the Farm, sir. You see, Grimes is a great hand at buying things uncommonly cheap, and selling 'em—uncommonly dear. To-day it seems—he was disappointed—"

"Ah?" said Bellew.

"At exactly—twenty-three minutes to six, sir," said the Sergeant, consulting his large silver watch, "I were sitting in my usual corner—beside the chimley, sir,—when in comes Grimes—like a thunder-cloud.—Calls for a pint of ale—in a tankard. Tom draws pint—which Tom is the landlord, sir. 'Buy anything at the sale, Mr. Grimes?' says Tom,—'Sale!' says Grimes, 'sale indeed!' and falls a cursing—folk up at the Farm—shocking—outrageous. Ends by threatening to foreclose mortgage—within the month. Upon which—I raise a protest—upon which he grows abusive,—upon which I was forced to pour his ale over him,—after which I ran him out into the road—and there it is, you see."

"And—he threatened to foreclose the mortgage on Dapplemere Farm, did he, Sergeant!"

"Within the month, sir!—upon which I warned him—inn parlour no place—lady's private money troubles—gaping crowd—dammit!"

"And so he is turning you out of his cottage?"

"Within the week, sir,—but then—beer down the neck—is rather unpleasant!" and here the Sergeant uttered a short laugh, and was immediately grave again. "It isn't," he went on, "it isn't as *I* mind the inconvenience of moving, sir—though I shall be mighty sorry to leave the old place, still, it isn't that so much as the small corner cup-board, and my bookshelf by the chimley. There never was such a cup-board,—no sir,—there never was a cup-board so well calculated to hold a pair o' jack boots, not to mention spurs, highlows, burnishers, shoulder-chains, polishing brushes, and—a boot-jack, as that same small corner cup-board. As for the book-shelf beside the chimley, sir—exactly three foot three,—sunk in a recess—height, the third button o' my coat,—capacity, fourteen books. You couldn't get another book on that shelf—no, not if you tried with a sledge-hammer, or a hydraulic engine. Which is highly surprising when you consider that fourteen books is the true, and exact number of books as I possess."

"Very remarkable!" said Bellew.

"Then again,—there's my comrade,—Peter Day (The Sergeant pronounced it as though it were all one word). Sir, my comrade Peterday is a very remarkable man,—most cobblers are. When he's not cobbling, he's reading,—when not reading, he's cobbling, or mending clocks, and watches, and, betwixt this and that, my comrade has picked up a power of information,—though he lost his leg a doing of it—in a gale of wind—off the Cape of Good Hope, for my comrade was a sailor, sir. Consequently he is a handy man, most sailors are and makes his own wooden legs, sir, he is also a musician—the tin whistle, sir,—and here we are!"

Saying which, the Sergeant halted, wheeled, opened a very small gate, and ushered Bellew into a very small garden bright with flowers, beyond which was a very small cottage indeed, through the open door of which there issued a most appetizing odour, accompanied by a whistle, wonderfully clear, and sweet, that was rendering "Tom Bowling" with many shakes, trills, and astonishing runs.

Peterday was busied at the fire with a long toasting-fork in his hand, but, on their entrance, breaking off his whistling in the very middle of a note, he sprang nimbly to his feet, (or rather, his foot), and stood revealed as a short, yet strongly built man, with a face that, in one way, resembled an island in that it was completely surrounded by hair, and whisker. But it was, in all respects, a vastly pleasant island to behold, despite the somewhat craggy prominences of chin, and nose, and brow. In other words, it was a pleasing face notwithstanding the fierce, thick eye-brows which were more than offset by the merry blue eyes, and the broad, humourous mouth below.

"Peterday," said the Sergeant, "Mr. Bel-lew!"

"Glad to see you sir," said the mariner, saluting the visitor with a quick bob of the head, and a backward scrape of the wooden leg. "You couldn't make port at a better time, sir,—and because why?—because the kettle's a biling, sir, the muffins is piping hot, and the shrimps is a-laying hove to, waiting to be took aboard, sir." Saying which, Peterday bobbed his head again, shook his wooden leg again, and turned away to reach another cup and saucer.

It was a large room for so small a cottage, and comfortably furnished, with a floor of red tile, and with a grate at one end well raised up from the hearth. Upon the hob a kettle sang murmurously, and on a trivet stood a plate whereon rose a tower of toasted muffins. A round table occupied the middle of the floor and was spread with a snowy cloth whereon cups and saucers were arranged, while in the midst stood a great bowl of shrimps.

Now above the mantel-piece, that is to say, to the left of it, and fastened to the wall, was a length of rope cunningly tied into what is called a "running bowline," above this, on a shelf specially contrived to hold it, was the model of a full-rigged ship that was—to all appearances—making excellent way of it, with every stitch of canvas set and drawing, alow and aloft; above this again, was a sextant, and a telescope. Opposite all these, upon the other side of the mantel, were a pair of stirrups, three pairs of spurs, two cavalry sabres, and a carbine, while between these objects, in the very middle of the chimney, uniting, as it were, the Army, and the Navy, was a portrait of Queen Victoria.

Bellew also noticed that each side of the room partook of the same characteristics, one being devoted to things nautical, the other to objects military. All this Bellew noticed while the soldier was brewing the tea, and the sailor was bestowing the last finishing touches to the muffins.

"It aren't often as we're honoured wi' company, sir," said Peterday, as they sat down, "is it, Dick?"

"No," answered the Sergeant, handing Bellew the shrimps.

"We ain't had company to tea," said Peterday, passing Bellew the muffins, "no, we ain't had company to tea since the last time Miss Anthea, and Miss Priscilla honoured us, have we, Dick?"

"Honoured us," said the Sergeant, nodding his head approvingly, "is the one, and only word for it, Peterday."

"And the last time was this day twelve months, sir,—because why?—because this day twelve months 'appened to be Miss Priscilla's birthday,—consequently to-day is her birthday, likewise,—wherefore the muffins, and wherefore the shrimps, sir, for they was this day to have once more graced our board, Mr. Bellew."

"Graced our board," said the Sergeant, nodding his head again, "'graced our board,' is the only expression for it, Peterday. But they disappointed us, Mr. Bellew, sir,—on account of the sale."

"Messmate," said Peterday, with a note of concern in his voice, "how's the wind?"

"Tolerable, comrade, tolerable!"

"Then—why forget the tea?"

"Tea!" said the Sergeant with a guilty start, "why—so I am!— Mr. Bellew sir,—your pardon!" and, forthwith he began to pour out the tea very solemnly, but with less precision of movement than usual, and with abstracted gaze.

"The Sergeant tells me you are a musician," said Bellew, as Peterday handed him another muffin.

"A musician,—me! think o' that now! To be sure, I do toot on the tin whistle now and then, sir, such things as 'The British Grenadiers,' and the 'Girl I left behind me,' for my shipmate, and 'The Bay o' Biscay,' and 'A Life on the Ocean Wave,' for myself,—but a musician, Lord! Ye see, sir," said Peterday, taking advantage of the Sergeant's abstraction, and whispering confidentially behind his muffin, "that messmate o' mine has such a high opinion o' my gifts as is fair over-powering, and a tin whistle is only a tin whistle, after all."

"And it is about the only instrument I could ever get the hang of," said Bellew.

"Why—do you mean as you play, sir?"

"Hardly that, but I make a good bluff at it."

"Why then,—I've got a couple o' very good whistles,—if you're so minded we might try a doo-et, sir, arter tea."

"With pleasure!" nodded Bellew. But, hereupon, Peterday noticing that the Sergeant ate nothing, leaned over and touched him upon the shoulder.

"How's the wind, now, Shipmate?" he enquired.

"Why so so, Peterday, fairish! fairish!" said the Sergeant, stirring his tea round and round, and with his gaze fixed upon the opposite wall.

"Then messmate,—why not a muffin, or even a occasional shrimp,—where be your appetite?"

"Peterday," said the Sergeant, beginning to stir his tea faster than ever, and with his eyes still fixed, "consequent upon disparaging remarks having been passed by one Grimes,—our landlord,—concerning them as should not be mentioned in a inn parlour—or anywhere else—by such as said Grimes,—I was compelled to pour—a tankard of beer—over said Grimes, our landlord,—this arternoon, Peterday, at exactly—twelve and a half minutes past six, by my watch,—which done,—I ran our landlord—out into the road, Peterday, say—half a minute later, which would make it precisely thirteen minutes after the hour. Consequent upon which, comrade—we have received our marching orders."

"What messmate, is it heave our anchor, you mean?"

"I mean, comrade—that on Saturday next, being the twenty-fifth instant,—we march out—bag and baggage—horse, foot, and artillery,—we evacuate our position—in face of superior force,—for good and all, comrade."

"Is that so, shipmate?"

"It's rough on you, Peterday—it's hard on you, I'll admit, but things were said, comrade—relative to—business troubles of one as we both respect, Peterday,—things was said as called for—beer down the neck,—and running out into the road, comrade. But it's rough on you, Peterday seeing as you—like the Hussars at Assuan—was never engaged, so to speak."

"Aye, aye, Shipmate, that does ketch me,—all aback, shipmate. Why Lord! I'd give a pound,—two pound—ah, ten!—just to have been astern of him wi' a rope's end,—though—come to think of it I'd ha' preferred a capstan-bar."

"Peterday," said the Sergeant removing his gaze from the wall with a jerk, "on the twenty-fifth instant we shall be—without a roof to cover us, and—all my doing. Peterday—what have you to say about it?"

"Say, messmate,—why that you and me, honouring, and respecting two ladies as deserves to be honoured, and respected, ain't going to let such a small thing as this here cottage come betwixt us, and our honouring and respecting of them two ladies. If, therefore, we are due to quit this anchorage, why then it's all hands to the windlass with a heave yo ho, and merrily! say I. Messmate,—my fist!" Hereupon, with a very jerky movement indeed, the Sergeant reached out his remaining arm, and the soldier and the sailor shook hands very solemnly over the muffins (already vastly diminished in number) with a grip that spoke much.

"Peterday,—you have lifted a load off my heart—I thank ye

comrade,—and spoke like a true soldier. Peterday—the muffins!"

So now the Sergeant, himself once more, fell to in turn, and they ate, and drank, and laughed, and talked, until the shrimps were all gone, and the muffins were things of the past.

And now, declining all Bellew's offers of assistance, the soldier and the sailor began washing, and drying, and putting away their crockery, each in his characteristic manner,—the Sergeant very careful and exact, while the sailor juggled cups and saucers with the sure-handed deftness that seems peculiar to nautical fingers.

"Yes, Peterday," said the Sergeant, hanging each cup upon its appointed nail, and setting each saucer solicitously in the space reserved for it on the small dresser, "since you have took our marching orders as you have took 'em, I am quite reconciled to parting with these here snug quarters, barring only—a book-shelf, and a cup-board."

"Cupboard!" returned Peterday with a snort of disdain, "why there never was such a ill-contrived, lubberly cupboard as that, in all the world; you can't get at it unless you lay over to port,—on account o' the clothes-press, and then hard a starboard,—on account o' the dresser,—and then it being in the darkest corner—"

"True Peterday, but then I'm used to it, and use is everything as you know,—I can lay my hand upon anything—in a minute —watch me!" Saying which, the Sergeant squeezed himself between the press and the dresser, opened the cupboard, and took thence several articles which he named, each in order.

"A pair o' jack-boots,—two brushes,—blacking,—and a burnisher." Having set these down, one by one, upon the dresser, he wheeled, and addressed himself to Bellew, as follows:

"Mr. Bellew, sir,—this evening being the anniversary of a certain—event, sir, I will ask you—to excuse me—while I make the necessary preparations—to honour this anniversary —as is ever my custom." As he ended, he dropped the two brushes, the blacking, and the burnisher inside the legs of the boots, picked them up with a sweep of the arm, and, turning short round, strode out into the little garden.

"A fine fellow is Dick, sir!" nodded Peterday, beginning to fill a long clay pipe, "Lord!—what a sailor he 'd ha' made, to be sure!—failing which he's as fine a soldier as ever was, or will be, with enough war-medals to fill my Sunday hat, sir. When he lost his arm they gave him the V.C., and his discharge, sir,—because why—because a soldier wi' one arm ain't any more good than a sailor wi' one leg, d'ye see. So they tried to discharge Dick, but—Lord love you!—they couldn't, sir,— because why?—because Dick were a soldier bred and born, and is as much a soldier to-day, as ever he was,—ah! and always will be—until he goes marching aloft,—like poor Tom Bowling,—until one as is General of all the armies, and Admiral of all the fleets as ever sailed, shall call the last muster roll, sir. At this present moment, sir," continued the sailor, lighting his pipe with a live coal from the fire, "my messmate is a-sitting to the leeward o' the plum tree outside, a polishing of his jack-boots,—as don't need polishing, and a burnishing of his spurs,—as don't need burnishing. And because why?— because he goes on guard, to-night, according to custom."

"On guard!" repeated Bellew, "I'm afraid I don't understand."

"Of course you don't, sir," chuckled Peterday, "well then, to-night he marches away—in full regimentals, sir,—to mount guard. And—where, do you suppose?—why, I'll tell you,— under Miss Priscilla's window! He gets there as the clock is striking eleven, and there he stays, a marching to and fro, until twelve o'clock. Which does him a world o' good, sir, and noways displeases Miss Priscilla,—because why?—because she don't know nothing whatever about it." Hereupon, Peterday rose, and crossing to a battered sea-man's chest in the corner, came back with three or four tin whistles which he handed to Bellew, who laid aside his pipe, and, having selected one, ran tentatively up and down the scale while Peterday listened attentive of ear, and beaming of face.

"Sir," said he, "what do you say to 'Annie Laurie' as a start—shall we give 'em 'Annie Laurie'?—very good!—ready?—go!"

Thus, George Bellew, American citizen, and millionaire, piped away on a tin whistle with all the gusto in the world,—introducing little trills, and flourishes, here and there, that fairly won the one-legged sailor's heart.

They had already "given 'em" three or four selections, each of which had been vociferously encored by Peterday, or Bellew,—and had just finished an impassioned rendering of the "Suwanee River," when the Sergeant appeared with his boots beneath his arm.

"Shipmate!" cried Peterday, flourishing his whistle, "did ye ever hear a tin whistle better played, or mellerer in tone?"

"Meller—is the only word for it, comrade,—and your playing sirs, is—artistic—though doleful. P'raps you wouldn't mind giving us something brighter—a rattling quick-step? P'raps you might remember one as begins:

'Some talk of Alexander
And some, of Hercules;'

if it wouldn't be troubling you too much?"

Forthwith they burst forth into "The British Grenadiers?" and never did tin whistles render the famous old tune with more fire, and dash. As the stirring notes rang out, the Sergeant, standing upon the hearth, seemed to grow taller, his broad chest expanded, his eyes glowed, a flush crept up into his cheek, and the whole man thrilled to the music as he had done, many a time and oft, in years gone by. As the last notes died away, he glanced down at the empty sleeve pinned across his breast, shook his head, and thanking them in a very gruff voice indeed, turned on his heel, and busied himself at his little cupboard. Peterday now rose, and set a jug together with three glasses upon the table, also spoons, and a lemon, keeping his "weather-eye" meanwhile, upon the kettle,—which last, condescending to boil obligingly, he rapped three times with his wooden leg.

"Right O, shipmate!" he cried, very much as though he had been hailing the "main-top," whereupon the Sergeant emerged from between the clothes-press and the dresser with a black bottle in his hand, which he passed over to Peterday who set about brewing what he called a "jorum o' grog," the savour of which filled the place with a right pleasant fragrance. And, when the glasses brimmed, each with a slice of lemon a-top,— the Sergeant solemnly rose.

"Mr. Bellew, and comrade," said he, lifting his glass, "I give you—Miss Priscilla!"

"God bless her!" said Peterday.

"Amen!" added Bellew. So the toast was drunk,—the glasses were emptied, re-filled, and emptied again,—this time more slowly, and, the clock striking nine, Bellew rose to take his leave. Seeing which, the Sergeant fetched his hat and stick, and volunteered to accompany him a little way. So when Bellew had shaken the sailor's honest hand, they set out together.

"Sergeant," said Bellew, after they had walked some distance, "I have a message for you."

"For me, sir?"

"From Miss Priscilla."

"From—indeed, sir!"

"She bid me tell you that—the peaches are riper to-night than ever they were."

The Sergeant seemed to find in this a subject for profound thought, and he strode on beside Bellew very silently, and with his eyes straight before him.

"That the peaches were riper,—to-night,—than ever they were?" said he at last.

"Yes, Sergeant."

"Riper!" said the Sergeant, as though turning this over in his mind.

"Riper than ever they were!" nodded Bellew.

"The—peaches, I think, sir?"

"The peaches, yes." Bellew heard the Sergeant's finger rasping to and fro across his shaven chin.

"Mr. Bellew, sir—she is a—very remarkable woman, sir!"

"Yes, Sergeant!"

"A—wonderful woman!"

"Yes, Sergeant!"

"The kind of woman that—improves with age, sir!"

"Yes, Sergeant."

"Talking of—peaches, sir, I've often thought—she is—very like a peach—herself, sir."

"Very, Sergeant, but—"

"Well, sir?"

"Peaches do—*not* improve with age, Sergeant,—'and the peaches are—riper than ever they were,—to-night!'" The Sergeant stopped short, and stared at Bellew wide-eyed.

"Why—sir," said he very slowly, "you don't mean to say you—think as she—meant—that—?"

"But I do!" nodded Bellew. And now, just as suddenly as he had stopped, the Sergeant turned, and went on again.

"Lord!" he whispered—"Lord! Lord!"

The moon was rising, and looking at the Sergeant, Bellew saw that there was a wonderful light in his face, yet a light that was not of the moon.

"Sergeant," said Bellew, laying a hand upon his shoulder, "why don't you speak to her?"

"Speak to her,—what me! No, no, Mr. Bellew!" said the Sergeant, hastily. "No, no,—can't be done, sir,—not to be mentioned, or thought of, sir!" The light was all gone out of his face, now, and he walked with his chin on his breast.

"The surprising thing to me, Sergeant, is that you have never thought of putting your fortune to the test, and—speaking your mind to her, before now."

"Thought of it, sir!" repeated the Sergeant, bitterly, "thought of it!—Lord, sir! I've thought of it—these five years—and more. I've thought of it—day and night. I've thought of it so very much that I know—I never can—speak my mind to her. Look at me!" he cried suddenly, wheeling and confronting Bellew, but not at all like his bold, erect, soldierly self,—"Yes, look at me,—a poor, battered, old soldier—with his—best arm gone,—left behind him in India, and with nothing in the world but his old uniform,—getting very frayed and worn,—

like himself, sir,—a pair o' jack boots, likewise very much worn, though wonderfully patched, here and there, by my good comrade, Peterday,—a handful of medals, and a very modest pension. Look at me, with the best o' my days behind me, and wi' only one arm left—and I'm a deal more awkward and helpless with that one arm than you'd think, sir,—look at me, and then tell me how could such a man dare to speak his mind to—such a woman. What right has—such a man to even think of speaking his mind to—such a woman, when there's part o' that man already in the grave? Why, no right, sir,—none in the world. Poverty, and one arm, are facts as make it impossible for that man to—ever speak his mind. And, sir—that man—never will. Sir,—good night to you!—and a pleasant walk!—I turn back here."

Which the Sergeant did, then and there, wheeling sharp right about face; yet, as Bellew watched him go, he noticed that the soldier's step was heavy, and slow, and it seemed that, for once, the Sergeant had even forgotten to put on his imaginary spurs.

CHAPTER XV

In which Adam explains

"Adam!"

"Yes, Miss Anthea."

"How much money did Mr. Bellew give you to—buy the furniture?"

Miss Anthea was sitting in her great elbow chair, leaning forward with her chin in her hand, looking at him in the way which always seemed to Adam as though she could see into the verimost recesses of his mind. Therefore Adam twisted his hat in his hands, and stared at the ceiling, and the floor, and the table before Miss Anthea, and the wall behind Miss Anthea— anywhere but at Miss Anthea.

"You ax me—how much it were, Miss Anthea?"

"Yes, Adam."

"Well,—it were a goodish sum."

"Was it—fifty pounds?"

"Fifty pound!" repeated Adam, in a tone of lofty disdain, "no, Miss Anthea, it were *not* fifty pound."

"Do you mean it was—more?"

"Ah!" nodded Adam, "I mean as it were a sight more. If you was to take the fifty pound you mention, add twenty more, and then another twenty to that, and then come ten more to that,—why then—you'd be a bit nigher the figure—"

"A hundred pounds!" exclaimed Anthea, aghast.

"Ah! a hundred pound!" nodded Adam, rolling the words upon his tongue with great gusto,—"one—hundred—pound, were the sum, Miss Anthea."

"Oh, Adam!"

"Lord love you, Miss Anthea!—that weren't nothing,—that were only a flea-bite, as you might say,—he give more—ah! nigh double as much as that for the side-board."

"Nonsense, Adam!"

"It be gospel true, Miss Anthea. That there sideboard were the plum o' the sale, so to speak, an' old Grimes had set 'is 'eart on it, d'ye see. Well, it were bid up to eighty-six pound, an' then Old Grimes 'e goes twenty more, making it a hundred an' six. Then—jest as I thought it were all over, an' jest as that there Old Grimes were beginning to swell hisself up wi' triumph, an' get that red in the face as 'e were a sight to behold,—Mr. Belloo, who'd been lightin' 'is pipe all this time, up and sez, —'Fifty up!' 'e sez in his quiet way, making it a hundred an' fifty-six pound, Miss Anthea,—which were too much for Grimes,—Lord! I thought as that there man were going to burst, Miss Anthea!" and Adam gave vent to his great laugh at the mere recollection. But Anthea was grave enough, and the troubled look in her eyes quickly sobered him.

"A hundred and fifty-six pounds!" she repeated in an awed voice, "but it—it is awful!"

"Steepish!" admitted Adam, "pretty steepish for a old sideboard, I'll allow, Miss Anthea,—but you see it were a personal matter betwixt Grimes an' Mr. Belloo. I began to think as they never would ha' left off biddin', an' by George!— I don't believe as Mr. Belloo ever would have left off biddin'. Ye see, there's summat about Mr. Belloo,—whether it be his voice, or his eye, or his chin,—I don't know,—but there be summat about him as says, very distinct that if so be 'e should 'appen to set 'is mind on a thing,—why 'e's a-going to get it, an' 'e ain't a-going to give in till 'e do get it. Ye see, Miss Anthea, 'e's so very quiet in 'is ways, an' speaks so soft, an' gentle,—p'raps that's it. Say, for instance, 'e were to ax you for summat, an' you said 'No'—well, 'e wouldn't make no fuss about it,—not 'im,—he'd jest—take it, that's what he'd do. As for that there sideboard he'd a sat there a bidding and a bidding all night I do believe."

"But, Adam, why did he do it! Why did he buy—all that furniture?"

"Well,—to keep it from being took away, p'raps!"

"Oh, Adam!—what am I to do?"

"Do, Miss Anthea?"

"The mortgage must be paid off—dreadfully soon—you know that, and—I can't—Oh, I can't give the money back—"

"Why—give it back!—No, a course not, Miss Anthea!"

"But I—can't—keep it!"

"Can't keep it, Miss Anthea mam,—an' why not?"

"Because I'm very sure he doesn't want all those things,—the idea is quite—absurd! And yet,—even if the hops do well, the money they bring will hardly be enough by itself, and so—I was selling my furniture to make it up, and—now—Oh! what am I to do?" and she leaned her head wearily upon her hand.

Now, seeing her distress, Adam all sturdy loyalty that he was, must needs sigh in sympathy, and fell, once more, to twisting his hat until he had fairly wrung it out of all semblance to its kind, twisting and screwing it between his strong hands as though he would fain wring out of it some solution to the problem that so perplexed his mistress. Then, all at once, the frown vanished from his brow, his grip loosened upon his unfortunate hat, and his eye brightened with a sudden gleam.

"Miss Anthea," said he, drawing a step nearer, and lowering his voice mysteriously, "supposing as I was to tell you that 'e did want that furnitur',—ah! an' wanted it bad?"

"Now how can he, Adam? It isn't as though he lived in England," said Anthea, shaking her head, "his home is thousands of miles away,—he is an American, and besides—"

"Ah!—but then—even a American—may get married. Miss Anthea, mam!" said Adam.

"Married!" she repeated, glancing up very quickly, "Adam— what do you mean?"

"Why you must know," began Adam, wringing at his hat again, "ever since the day I found him asleep in your hay, Miss Anthea, mam, Mr. Belloo has been very kind, and—friendly like. Mr. Belloo an' me 'ave smoked a good many sociable pipes together, an' when men smoke together, Miss Anthea, they likewise talk together."

"Yes?—Well?" said Anthea, rather breathlessly, and taking up a pencil that happened to be lying near to hand.

"And Mr. Belloo," continued Adam, heavily, "Mr. Belloo has done me—the—the honour," here Adam paused to give an extra twist to his hat,—"the—honour, Miss Anthea—"

"Yes, Adam."

"Of confiding to me 'is 'opes—" said Adam slowly, finding it much harder to frame his well-meaning falsehood than he had supposed, "his—H-O-P-E-S—'opes, Miss Anthea, of settling down very soon, an' of marryin' a fine young lady as 'e 'as 'ad 'is eye on a goodish time,—'aving knowed her from childhood's hour, Miss Anthea, and as lives up to Lonnon—"

"Yes—Adam!"

"Consequently—'e bought all your furnitur' to set up 'ousekeepin', don't ye see."

"Yes,—I see, Adam!" Her voice was low, soft and gentle as ever, but the pencil was tracing meaningless scrawls in her shaking fingers.

"So you don't 'ave to be no-wise back-ard about keepin' the money, Miss Anthea."

"Oh no,—no, of course not, I—I understand, it was—just a—business transaction."

"Ah!—that's it,—a business transaction!" nodded Adam, "So you'll put the money a one side to help pay off the mortgage, eh, Miss Anthea?"

"Yes."

"If the 'ops comes up to what they promise to come up to, —you'll be able to get rid of Old Grimes—for good an' all, Miss Anthea."

"Yes, Adam."

"An' you be quite easy in your mind, now, Miss Anthea—about keepin' the money?"

"Quite!—Thank you, Adam—for—telling me. You can go now."

"Why then—Good-night! Miss Anthea, mam,—the mortgage is as good as paid,—there ain't no such 'ops nowhere near so good as our'n be. An'—you're quite free o' care, an' 'appy 'earted, Miss Anthea?"

"Quite—Oh quite, Adam!"

But when Adam's heavy tread had died away,—when she was all alone, she behaved rather strangely for one so free of care, and happy-hearted. Something bright and glistening splashed upon the paper before her, the pencil slipped from her fingers, and, with a sudden, choking cry, she swayed forward, and hid her face in her hands.

CHAPTER XVI

In which Adam proposes a game

"To be, or not to be!" Bellew leaned against the mighty hole of "King Arthur," and stared up at the moon with knitted brows. "That is the question!—whether I shall brave the slings, and arrows and things, and—speak tonight, and have done with it—one way or another, or live on, a while, secure in this uncertainty? To wait? Whether I shall, at this so early stage, pit all my chances of happiness against the chances of—losing her, and with her—Small Porges, bless him! and all the quaint, and lovable beings of this wonderful Arcadia of mine. For, if her answer be 'No,'—what recourse have I,—what is there left me but to go wandering forth again, following the wind, and with the gates of Arcadia shut upon me for ever? 'To be, or not to be,—that is the question!'"

"Be that you, Mr. Belloo, sir?"

"Even so, Adam. Come sit ye a while, good knave, and gaze upon Dian's loveliness, and smoke, and let us converse of dead kings."

"Why, kings ain't much in my line, sir,—living or dead uns, —me never 'aving seen any—except a pic'ter,—and that tore, though very life like. But why I were a lookin' for you was to ax you to back me up,—an' to—play the game, Mr. Belloo sir."

"Why—as to that, my good Adam,—my gentle Daphnis, —my rugged Euphemio,—you may rely upon me to the uttermost. Are you in trouble? Is it counsel you need, or only money? Fill your pipe, and, while you smoke, confide your cares to me,—put me wise, or, as your French cousins would say,—make me 'au fait.'"

"Well," began Adam, when his pipe was well alight, "in the first place, Mr. Belloo sir, I begs to remind you, as Miss Anthea sold her furnitur' to raise enough money as with what the 'ops will bring, might go to pay off the mortgage,—for good an' all, sir."

"Yes."

"Well, to-night, sir, Miss Anthea calls me into the parlour to ax,—or as you might say,—en-quire as to the why, an' likewise the wherefore of you a buyin' all that furnitur'."

"Did she, Adam?"

"Ah!—'why did 'e do it?' says she—'well, to keep it from bein' took away, p'raps,' says I—sharp as any gimblet, sir."

"Good!" nodded Bellew.

"Ah!—but it weren't no good, sir," returned Adam, "because she sez as 'ow your 'ome being in America, you couldn't really need the furnitur',—nor yet want the furnitur',—an' blest if she wasn't talkin' of handing you the money back again."

"Hum!" said Bellew.

"Seeing which, sir, an' because she must have that money if she 'opes to keep the roof of Dapplemere over 'er 'ead, I, there an' then, made up,—or as you might say,—concocted a story, a anecdote, or a yarn,—upon the spot, Mr. Belloo sir."

"Most excellent Machiavelli!—proceed!"

"I told her, sir, as you bought that furnitur' on account of you being wishful to settle down,—whereat she starts, an' looks at me wi' her eyes big, an' surprised-like. I told 'er, likewise, as you had told me on the quiet,—or as you might say,—confidential, that you bought that furnitur' to set up 'ouse-keeping on account o' you being on the p'int o' marrying a fine young lady up to Lonnon,—"

"What!" Bellew didn't move, nor did he raise his voice, —nevertheless Adam started back, and instinctively threw up his arm.

"You—told her—that?"

"I did sir."

"But you knew it was a—confounded lie."

"Aye,—I knowed it. But I'd tell a hundred,—ah! thousands o' lies, con-founded, or otherwise,—to save Miss Anthea."

"To save her?"

"From ruination, sir! From losing Dapplemere Farm, an' every thing she has in the world. Lord love ye!—the 'ops can never bring in by theirselves all the three thousand pounds as is owing,—it ain't to be expected,—but if that three thousand pound ain't paid over to that dirty Grimes by next Saturday week as ever was, that dirty Grimes turns Miss Anthea out o' Dapplemere, wi' Master Georgy, an' poor little Miss Priscilla, —An' what'll become o' them then,—I don't know. Lord! when I think of it the 'Old Adam' do rise up in me to that extent as I'm minded to take a pitch-fork and go and skewer that there Grimes to his own chimbley corner. Ye see Mr. Belloo sir," he went on, seeing Bellew was silent still, "Miss Anthea be that proud, an' independent that she'd never ha' took your money, sir, if I hadn't told her that there lie,—so that's why I did tell her that here lie."

"I see," nodded Bellew, "I see!—yes,—you did quite right. You acted for the best, and you—did quite right, Adam,—yes, quite right"

"Thankee sir!"

"And so—this is the game I am to play, is it?"

"That's it, sir; if she ax's you,—'are you goin' to get married?' —you'll tell her 'yes,—to a lady as you've knowed from your childhood's hour,—living in Lonnon,'—that's all, sir."

"That's all is it, Adam!" said Bellew slowly, turning to look up at the moon again. "It doesn't sound very much, does it? Well, I'll play your game,—Adam,—yes, you may depend upon me."

"Thankee, Mr. Belloo sir,—thankee sir!—though I do 'ope as you'll excuse me for taking such liberties, an' making so free wi' your 'eart, and your affections, sir?"

"Oh certainly, Adam!—the cause excuses—everything."

"Then, good-night, sir!"

"Good-night, Adam!"

So this good, well-meaning Adam strode away, proud on the whole of his night's work, leaving Bellew to frown up at the moon with teeth clenched tight upon his pipe-stem.

CHAPTER XVII

How Bellew began the game

Now in this life of ours, there be games of many, and divers, sorts, and all are calculated to try the nerve, courage, or skill of the player, as the case may be. Bellew had played many kinds of games in his day, and, among others, had once been famous as a Eight Tackle on the Harvard Eleven. Upon him he yet bore certain scars received upon a memorable day when Yale, flushed with success, saw their hitherto invincible line rent and burst asunder, saw a figure torn, bruised, and bleeding, flash out and away down the field to turn defeat into victory, and then to be borne off honourably to hospital, and bed.

If Bellew thought of this, by any chance, as he sat there, staring up at the moon, it is very sure that, had the choice been given him, he would joyfully have chosen the game of torn flesh, and broken bones, or any other game, no matter how desperate, rather than this particular game that Adam had invented, and thrust upon him.

Presently Bellew knocked the ashes from his pipe, and rising, walked on slowly toward the house. As he approached, he heard someone playing the piano, and the music accorded well with his mood, or his mood with the music, for it was haunting, and very sweet, and with a recurring melody in a minor key, that seemed to voice all the sorrow of Humanity, past, present, and to come.

Drawn by the music, he crossed the Rose Garden, and reaching the terrace, paused there; for the long French windows were open, and, from where he stood, he could see Anthea seated at the piano. She was dressed in a white gown of some soft, clinging material, and among the heavy braids of her hair was a single great, red rose. And, as he watched, he thought she had never looked more beautiful than now, with the soft glow of the candles upon her; for her face reflected the tender sadness of the music, it was in the mournful droop of her scarlet lips, and the sombre depths of her eyes. Close beside her sat little Miss Priscilla busy with her needle as usual, but now she paused, and lifting her head in her quick, bird-like way, looked up at Anthea, long, and fixedly.

"Anthea my dear," said she suddenly, "I'm fond of music, and I love to hear you play, as you know,—but I never heard you play quite so—dolefully? dear me, no,—that's not the right word,—nor dismal,—but I mean something between the two."

"I thought you were fond of Grieg, Aunt Priscilla."

"So I am, but then, even in his gayest moments, poor Mr. Grieg was always breaking his heart over something, or other. And—Gracious!—there's Mr. Bellew at the window. Pray come in, Mr. Bellew, and tell us how you liked Peterday, and the muffins?"

"Thank you!" said Bellew, stepping in through the long French window, "but I should like to hear Miss Anthea play again, first, if she will?"

But Anthea, who had already risen from the piano, shook her head:

"I only play when I feel like it,—to please myself,—and Aunt Priscilla," said she, crossing to the broad, low window-seat, and leaning out into the fragrant night.

"Why then," said Bellew, sinking into the easy-chair that Miss Priscilla indicated with a little stab of her needle, "why then the muffins were delicious, Aunt Priscilla, and Peterday was just exactly what a one-legged mariner ought to be."

"And the shrimps, Mr. Bellew?" enquired Miss Priscilla, busy at her sewing again.

"Out-shrimped all other shrimps so ever!" he answered, glancing to where Anthea sat with her chin propped in her hand, gazing up at the waning moon, seemingly quite oblivious of him.

"And did—*He*—pour out the tea?" enquired Miss Priscilla, "from the china pot with the blue flowers and the Chinese Mandarin fanning himself,—and very awkward, of course, with his one hand,—I don't mean the Mandarin, Mr. Bellew, —and very full of apologies?"

"He did."

"Just as usual; yes he always does,—and every year he gives me three lumps of sugar,—and I only take one, you know. It's a pity," sighed Miss Priscilla, "that it was his right arm,—a great pity!" And here she sighed again, and, catching herself, glanced up quickly at Bellew, and smiled to see how completely absorbed he was in contemplation of the silent figure in the window-seat. "But, after all, better a right arm—than a leg," she pursued,—"at least, I think so!"

"Certainly!" murmured Bellew.

"A man with only one leg, you see, would be almost as helpless as an—old woman with a crippled foot,—"

"Who grows younger, and brighter, every year!" added Bellew, turning to her with his pleasant smile, "yes, and I think, —prettier!"

"Oh, Mr. Bellew!" exclaimed Miss Priscilla shaking her head at him reprovingly, yet looking pleased, none the less,—"how can you be so ridiculous,—Good gracious me!"

"Why, it was the Sergeant who put it into my head,—"

"The Sergeant?"

"Yes,—it was after I had given him your message about peaches, Aunt Priscilla and—"

"Oh dear heart!" exclaimed Miss Priscilla, at this juncture, "Prudence is out, to-night, and I promised to bake the bread for her, and here I sit chatting, and gossipping while that bread goes rising, and rising all over the kitchen!" And Miss Priscilla laid aside her sewing, and catching up her stick, hurried to the door.

"And I was almost forgetting to wish you 'many happy returns of the day, Aunt Priscilla!'" said Bellew, rising.

At this familiar appellation, Anthea turned sharply, in time to see him stoop, and kiss Miss Priscilla's small, white hand; whereupon Anthea must needs curl her lip at his broad back. Then he opened the door, and Miss Priscilla tapped away, even more quickly than usual.

Anthea was half-sitting, half-kneeling among the cushions in the corner of the deep window, apparently still lost in contemplation of the moon. So much so, that she did not stir, or even lower her up-ward gaze, when Bellew came, and stood beside her.

Therefore, taking advantage of the fixity of her regard, he, once more, became absorbed in her loveliness. Surely a most unwise proceeding—in Arcadia, by the light of a midsummer moon! And he mentally contrasted the dark, proud beauty of her face, with that of all the women he had ever known,—to their utter, and complete disparagement.

"Well?" enquired Anthea, at last, perfectly conscious of his look, and finding the silence growing irksome, yet still with her eyes averted,—"Well, Mr. Bellew?"

"On the contrary," he answered, "the moon is on the wane!"

"The moon!" she repeated, "Suppose it is,—what then?"

"True happiness can only come riding astride the full moon you know,—you remember old Nannie told us so."

"And you—believed it?" she enquired scornfully.

"Why, of course!" he answered in his quiet way.

Anthea didn't speak but, once again, the curl of her lip was eloquent.

"And so," he went on, quite unabashed, "when I behold Happiness riding astride the full moon, I shall just reach up, in the most natural manner in the world, and—take it down, that it may abide with me, world without end."

"Do you think you will be tall enough?"

"We shall see,—when the time comes."

"I think it's all very ridiculous!" said Anthea.

"Why then—suppose you play for me, that same, plaintive piece you were playing as I came in,—something of Grieg's I think it was,—will you, Miss Anthea?"

She was on the point of refusing, then, as if moved by some capricious whim, she crossed to the piano, and dashed into the riotous music of a Polish Dance. As the wild notes leapt beneath her quick, brown fingers, Bellew, seated near-by, kept his eyes upon the great, red rose in her hair, that nodded slyly at him with her every movement. And surely, in all the world, there had never bloomed a more tantalizing, more wantonly provoking rose than this! Wherefore Bellew, very wisely, turned his eyes from its glowing temptation. Doubtless observing which, the rose, in evident desperation, nodded, and swayed, until, it had fairly nodded itself from its sweet resting-place, and, falling to the floor, lay within Bellew's reach. Whereupon, he promptly stooped, and picked it up, and, —even as, with a last, crashing chord, Anthea ceased playing, and turned, in that same moment he dropped it deftly into his coat pocket.

"Oh! by the way, Mr. Bellew," she said, speaking as if the idea had but just entered her mind, "what do you intend to do about—all your furniture?"

"Do about it?" he repeated, settling the rose carefully in a corner of his pocket where it would not be crushed by his pipe.

"I mean—where would you like it—stored until you can send, and have it—taken away?"

"Well,—I—er—rather thought of keeping it—where it was if you didn't mind."

"I'm afraid that will be—impossible, Mr. Bellew."

"Why then the barn will be an excellent place for it, I don't suppose the rats and mice will do it any real harm, and as for the damp, and the dust—"

"Oh! you know what I mean!" exclaimed Anthea, beginning to tap the floor impatiently with her foot. "Of course we can't go on using the things now that they are your property, it —wouldn't be—right."

"Very well," he nodded, his fingers questing anxiously after the rose again, "I'll get Adam to help me to shift it all into the barn, to-morrow morning."

"Will you please be serious, Mr. Bellew!"

"As an owl!" he nodded.

"Why then—of course you will be leaving Dapplemere soon, and I should like to know exactly when, so that I can—make the necessary arrangements."

"But you see, I am not leaving Dapplemere soon or even thinking of it."

"Not?" she repeated, glancing up at him in swift surprise.

"Not until—you bid me."

"I?"

"You!"

"But I—I understood that you—intend to—settle down?"

"Certainly!" nodded Bellew, transferring his pipe to another pocket altogether, lest it should damage the rose's tender petals. "To settle down has lately become the—er—ambition of my life."

"Then pray," said Anthea, taking up a sheet of music, and beginning to study it with attentive eyes, "be so good as to tell me—what you mean."

"That necessarily brings us back to the moon again," answered Bellew.

"The moon?"

"The moon!"

"But what in the world has the moon to do with your furniture?" she demanded, her foot beginning to tap again.

"Everything!—I bought that furniture with—er—with one eye on the moon, as it were,—consequently the furniture, the moon, and I, are bound indissolubly together."

"You are pleased to talk in riddles, to-night, and really, Mr. Bellew, I have no time to waste over them, so, if you will excuse me—"

"Thank you for playing to me," he said, as he held the door open for her.

"I played because I—I felt like it, Mr. Bellew."

"Nevertheless, I thank you."

"When you make up your mind about—the furniture,—please let me know."

"When the moon is at the full, yes."

"Can it be possible that you are still harping on the wild words of poor old Nannie?" she exclaimed, and once more, she curled her lip at him.

"Nannie is very old, I'll admit," he nodded, "but surely you remember that we proved her right in one particular,—I mean about the Tiger Mark, you know."

Now, when he said this, for no apparent reason, the eyes that had hitherto been looking into his, proud and scornful, —wavered, and were hidden under their long, thick lashes; the colour flamed in her cheeks, and, without another word, she was gone.

CHAPTER XVIII

How the Sergeant went upon his guard

The Arcadians, one and all, generally follow that excellent maxim which runs:

"Early to bed, and early to rise Makes a man healthy, and wealthy, and wise."

Healthy they are, beyond a doubt, and, in their quaint, simple fashion, profoundly wise. If they are not extraordinarily wealthy, yet are they generally blessed with contented minds which, after all, is better than money, and far more to be desired than fine gold.

Now whether their general health, happiness, and wisdom is to be attributed altogether to their early to bed proclivities, is perhaps a moot question. Howbeit, to-night, long after these weary Arcadians had forgotten their various cares, and troubles in the blessed oblivion of sleep, (for even Arcadia has its troubles) Bellew sat beneath the shade of "King Arthur" alone with his thoughts.

Presently, however, he was surprised to hear the house-door open, and close very softly, and to behold—not the object of his meditations, but Miss Priscilla coming towards him.

As she caught sight of him in the shadow of the tree, she stopped and stood leaning upon her stick as though she were rather disconcerted.

"Aunt Priscilla!" said he, rising.

"Oh!—it's you?" she exclaimed, just as though she hadn't known it all along. "Dear me! Mr. Bellew,—how lonely you look, and dreadfully thoughtful,—good gracious!" and she glanced up at him with her quick, girlish smile. "I suppose you are wondering what I am doing out here at this unhallowed time of night—it must be nearly eleven o'clock. Oh dear me!—yes you are!—Well, sit down, and I'll tell you. Let us sit here,—in the darkest corner,—there. Dear heart!—how bright the moon is to be sure." So saying, Miss Priscilla ensconced herself at the very end of the rustic bench, where the deepest shadow lay.

"Well, Mr. Bellew," she began, "as you know, to-day is my birthday. As to my age, I am—let us say,—just turned twenty-one and, being young, and foolish, Mr. Bellew, I have come out here to watch another very foolish person,—a ridiculous, old Sergeant of Hussars, who will come marching along, very soon, to mount guard in full regimentals, Mr. Bellew,—with his busby on his head, with his braided tunic and dolman, and his great big boots, and with his spurs jingling, and his sabre bright under the moon."

"So then—you know he comes?"

"Why of course I do. And I love to hear the jingle of his spurs, and to watch the glitter of his sabre. So, every year, I come here, and sit among the shadows, where he can't see me, and watch him go march, march, marching up and down, and to and fro, until the clock strikes twelve, and he goes marching home again. Oh dear me!—it's all very foolish, of course,—but I love to hear the jingle of his spurs."

"And—have you sat here watching him, every year?"

"Every year!"

"And he has never guessed you were watching him?"

"Good gracious me!—of course not."

"Don't you think, Aunt Priscilla, that you are—just a little—cruel?"

"Cruel—why—what do you mean?"

"I gave him your message, Aunt Priscilla."

"What message?"

"That 'to-night, the peaches were riper than ever they were.'"

"Oh!" said Miss Priscilla, and waited expectantly for Bellew to continue. But, as he was silent she glanced at him, and seeing him staring at the moon, she looked at it, also. And after she had gazed for perhaps half a minute, as Bellew was still silent, she spoke, though in a very small voice indeed.

"And—what did—he say?"

"Who?" enquired Bellew.

"Why the—the Sergeant, to be sure."

"Well, he gave me to understand that a poor, old soldier with only one arm left him, must be content to stand aside, always and—hold his peace, just because he was a poor, maimed, old soldier. Don't you think that you have been—just a little cruel—all these years, Aunt Priscilla?"

"Sometimes—one is cruel—only to be—kind!" she answered.

"Aren't the peaches ripe enough, after all, Aunt Priscilla?"

"Over-ripe!" she said bitterly, "Oh—they are over-ripe!"

"Is that all, Aunt Priscilla?"

"No," she answered, "no, there's—this!" and she held up her little crutch stick.

"Is that all, Aunt Priscilla?"

"Oh!—isn't—that enough?" Bellew rose. "Where are you going—What are you going to do?" she demanded.

"Wait!" said he, smiling down at her perplexity, and so he turned, and crossed to a certain corner of the orchard. When he came back he held out a great, glowing peach towards her.

"You were quite right," he nodded, "it was so ripe that it fell at a touch."

But, as he spoke, she drew him down beside her in the shadow:

"Hush!" she whispered, "Listen!"

Now as they sat there, very silent,—faint and far-away upon the still night air, they heard a sound; a silvery, rhythmic sound, it was,—like the musical clash of fairy cymbals which drew rapidly nearer, and nearer; and Bellew felt that Miss Priscilla's hand was trembling upon his arm as she leaned forward, listening with a smile upon her parted lips, and a light in her eyes that was ineffably tender.

Nearer came the sound, and nearer, until, presently, now in moonlight, now in shadow, there strode a tall, martial figure in all the glory of braided tunic, and furred dolman, the three chevrons upon his sleeve, and many shining medals upon his breast,—a stalwart, soldierly figure, despite the one empty sleeve, who moved with the long, swinging stride that only the cavalry-man can possess. Being come beneath a certain latticed window, the Sergeant halted, and, next moment, his glittering sabre flashed up to the salute; then, with it upon his shoulder, he wheeled, and began to march up and down, his spurs jingling, his sabre gleaming, his dolman swinging, his sabre glittering, each time he wheeled; while Miss Priscilla leaning forward, watched him wide-eyed, and with hands tight clasped. Then, all at once,—with a little fluttering sigh she rose.

Thus, the Sergeant as he marched to and fro, was suddenly aware of one who stood in the full radiance of the moon,—and with one hand outstretched towards him. And now, as he paused, disbelieving his very eyes, he saw that in her extended hand she held a great ripe peach.

"Sergeant!" she said, speaking almost in a whisper, "Oh Sergeant—won't you—take it?"

The heavy sabre thudded down into the grass, and he took a sudden step towards her. But, even now, he hesitated, until, coming nearer yet, he could look down into her eyes.

Then he spoke, and his voice was very hoarse, and uneven:

"Miss Priscilla?" he said, "Priscilla?—Oh, Priscilla!" And, with the word, he had fallen on his knees at her feet, and his strong, solitary arm was folded close about her.

CHAPTER XIX

In which Porges Big, and Porges Small discuss the subject of Matrimony

"What is it, my Porges?"

"Well,—I'm a bit worried, you know."

"Worried?"

"Yes,—'fraid I shall be an old man before my time, Uncle Porges. Adam says it's worry that ages a man,—an' it killed a cat too!"

"And why do you worry?"

"Oh, it's my Auntie Anthea, a course!—she was crying again last night—"

"Crying!" Bellew had been lying flat upon his back in the fragrant shadow of the hay-rick, but now he sat up—very suddenly, so suddenly that Small Porges started. "Crying!" he repeated, "last night! Are you sure?"

"Oh yes! You see, she forgot to come an' 'tuck me up' last night, so I creeped downstairs,—very quietly, you know, to see why. An' I found her bending over the table, all sobbing, an' crying. At first she tried to pretend that she wasn't, but I saw the tears quite plain,—her cheeks were all wet, you know; an' when I put my arms round her—to comfort her a bit, an' asked her what was the matter, she only kissed me a lot, an' said 'nothing! nothing,—only a headache!'"

"And why was she crying, do you suppose, my Porges?"

"Oh!—money, a course!" he sighed.

"What makes you think it was money?"

"Cause she'd been talking to Adam,—I heard him say 'Goodnight,' as I creeped down the stairs,—"

"Ah?" said Bellew, staring straight before him. His beloved pipe had slipped from his fingers, and, for a wonder, lay all neglected. "It was after she had talked with Adam, was it, my Porges?"

"Yes,—that's why I knew it was 'bout money; Adam's always talking 'bout morgyges, an' bills, an' money. Oh Uncle Porges, how I do—hate money!"

"It is sometimes a confounded nuisance!" nodded Bellew.

"But I do wish we had some,—so we could pay all her bills, an' morgyges for her. She'd be so happy, you know, an' go about singing like she used to,—an' I shouldn't worry myself into an old man before my time,—all wrinkled, an' gray, you know; an' all would be revelry, an' joy, if only she had enough gold, an' bank-notes!"

"And she was—crying, you say!" demanded Bellew again, his gaze still far away.

"Yes."

"You are quite sure you saw the—tears, my Porges?"

"Oh yes! an' there was one on her nose, too,—a big one, that shone awful' bright,—twinkled, you know."

"And she said it was only a headache, did she?"

"Yes, but that meant money,—money always makes her head ache, lately. Oh Uncle Porges!—I s'pose people do find fortunes, sometimes, don't they?"

"Why yes, to be sure they do."

"Then I wish I knew where they looked for them," said he with a very big sigh indeed, "I've hunted an' hunted in all the attics, an' the cupboards, an' under hedges, an' in ditches, an' prayed, an' prayed, you know,—every night."

"Then, of course, you'll be answered, my Porges."

"Do you really s'pose I shall be answered? You see it's such an awful' long way for one small prayer to have to go,—from here to heaven. An' there's clouds that get in the way; an' I'm 'fraid my prayers aren't quite big, or heavy enough, an' get lost, an' blown away in the wind."

"No, my Porges," said Bellew, drawing his arm about the small disconsolate figure, "you may depend upon it that your prayers fly straight up into heaven, and that neither the clouds, nor the wind can come between, or blow them away. So just keep on praying, old chap, and when the time is ripe, they'll be answered, never fear."

"Answered?—Do you mean,—oh Uncle Porges!—do you mean—the Money Moon?" The small hand upon Bellew's arm, quivered, and his voice trembled with eagerness.

"Why yes, to be sure,—the Money Moon, my Porges,—it's bound to come, one of these fine nights."

"Ah!—but when,—oh! when will the Money Moon ever come?"

"Well, I can't be quite sure, but I rather fancy, from the look of things, my Porges, that it will be pretty soon."

"Oh, I do hope so!—for her sake, an' my sake. You see, she may go getting herself married to Mr. Cassilis, if something doesn't happen soon, an' I shouldn't like that, you know."

"Neither should I, my Porges. But what makes you think so?"

"Why he's always bothering her, an' asking her to, you see. She always says 'No' a course, but—one of these fine days, I'm 'fraid she'll say 'Yes'—accidentally, you know."

"Heaven forbid, nephew!"

"Does that mean you hope not?"

"Indeed yes."

"Then I say heaven forbid, too,—'cause I don't think she'd ever be happy in Mr. Cassilis's great, big house. An' I shouldn't either."

"Why, of course not!"

"*You* never go about asking people to marry you, do you Uncle Porges!"

"Well, it could hardly be called a confirmed habit of mine."

"That's one of the things I like about you so,—all the time you've been here you haven't asked my Auntie Anthea once, have you?"

"No, my Porges,—not yet."

"Oh!—but you don't mean that you—ever will?"

"Would you be very grieved, and angry, if I did,—some day

soon, my Porges?"

"Well, I—I didn't think you were that kind of a man!" answered Small Porges, sighing and shaking his head regretfully.

"I'm afraid I am, nephew."

"Do you really mean that you want to—marry my Auntie Anthea?"

"I do."

"As much as Mr. Cassilis does?"

"A great deal more, I think."

Small Porges sighed again, and shook his head very gravely indeed:

"Uncle Porges," said he, "I'm—s'prised at you!"

"I rather feared you would be, nephew."

"It's all so awful' silly, you know!—why do you want to marry her?"

"Because, like a Prince in a fairy tale, I'm—er—rather anxious to—live happy ever after."

"Oh!" said Small Porges, turning this over in his mind, "I never thought of that."

"Marriage is a very important institution, you see, my Porges,—especially in this case, because I can't possibly live happy ever after, unless I marry—first—now can I?"

"No, I s'pose not!" Small Porges admitted, albeit reluctantly, after he had pondered the matter a while with wrinkled brow, "but why pick out—my Auntie Anthea?"

"Just because she happens to be your Auntie Anthea, of course."

Small Porges sighed again:

"Why then, if she's got to be married some day, so she can live happy ever after,—well,—I s'pose you'd better take her, Uncle Porges."

"Thank you, old chap,—I mean to."

"I'd rather you took her than Mr. Cassilis, an'—why there he is!"

"Who?"

"Mr. Cassilis. An' he's stopped, an' he's twisting his mestache."

Mr. Cassilis, who had been crossing the paddock, had indeed stopped, and was twisting his black moustache, as if he were hesitating between two courses. Finally, he pushed open the gate, and, approaching Bellew, saluted him with that supercilious air which Miss Priscilla always declared she found so "trying."

"Ah, Mr. Bellew! what might it be this morning,—the pitchfork—the scythe, or the plough?" he enquired.

"Neither, sir,—this morning it is—matrimony!"

"Eh!—I beg your pardon,—matrimony?"

"With a large M, sir," nodded Bellew, "marriage, sir, —wedlock; my nephew and I are discussing it in its aspects philosophical, sociological, and—"

"That is surely rather a—peculiar subject to discuss with a

child, Mr. Bellew—"

"Meaning my nephew, sir?"

"I mean—young George, there."

"Precisely,—my nephew, Small Porges."

"I refer," said Mr. Cassilis, with slow, and crushing emphasis, "to Miss Devine's nephew—"

"And mine, Mr. Cassilis,—mine by—er—mutual adoption, and inclination."

"And I repeat that your choice of subjects is—peculiar, to say the least of it."

"But then, mine is rather a peculiar nephew, sir. But, surely it was not to discuss nephews,—mine or anyone else's, that you are hither come, and our ears do wait upon you,—pray be seated, sir."

"Thank you, I prefer to stand."

"Strange!" murmured Bellew, shaking his head, "I never stand if I can sit, or sit if I can lie down."

"I should like you to define, exactly, your position—here at Dapplemere, Mr. Bellew."

Bellew's sleepy glance missed nothing of the other's challenging attitude, and his ear, nothing of Mr. Cassilis's authoritative tone, therefore his smile was most engaging as he answered:

"My position here, sir, is truly the most—er—enviable in the world. Prudence is an admirable cook,—particularly as regard Yorkshire Pudding; gentle, little Miss Priscilla is the most—er Aunt-like, and perfect of housekeepers; and Miss Anthea is our sovereign lady, before whose radiant beauty, Small Porges and I like true knights, and gallant gentles, do constant homage, and in whose behalf Small Porges and I do stand prepared to wage stern battle, by day, or by night."

"Indeed!" said Mr. Cassilis, and his smile was even more supercilious than usual.

"Yes, sir," nodded Bellew, "I do confess me a most fortunate, and happy, wight who, having wandered hither and yon upon this planet of ours, which is so vast, and so very small,—has, by the most happy chance, found his way hither into Arcady."

"And—may I enquire how long you intend to lead this Arcadian existence?"

"I fear I cannot answer that question until the full o' the moon, sir,—at present, I grieve to say,—I do not know."

Mr. Cassilis struck his riding-boot a sudden smart rap with his whip; his eyes snapped, and his nostrils dilated, as he glanced down into Bellew's imperturbable face.

"At least you know, and will perhaps explain, what prompted you to buy all that furniture? You were the only buyer at the sale I understand."

"Who—bought anything, yes," nodded Bellew.

"And pray—what was your object,—you—a stranger?"

"Well," replied Bellew slowly, as he began to fill his pipe, "I bought it because it was there to buy, you know; I bought it because furniture is apt to be rather useful, now and then,—I acquired the chairs to—er—sit in, the tables to—er—put things on, and—"

"Don't quibble with me, Mr. Bellew!"

"I beg your pardon, Mr. Cassilis!"

"When I ask a question, sir, I am in the habit of receiving a direct reply,—"

"And when I am asked a question, Mr. Cassilis, I am in the habit of answering it precisely as I please,—or not at all."

"Mr. Bellew, let me impress upon you, once and for all, that Miss Devine has friends,—old and tried friends, to whom she can always turn for aid in any financial difficulty she may have to encounter,—friends who can more than tide over all her difficulties without the—interference of strangers; and, as one of her oldest friends, I demand to know by what right you force your wholly unnecessary assistance upon her?"

"My very good sir," returned Bellew, shaking his head in gentle reproof, "really, you seem to forget that you are not addressing one of your grooms, or footmen,—consequently you force me to remind you of the fact; furthermore,—"

"That is no answer!" said Mr. Cassilis, his gloved hands tight-clenched upon his hunting-crop,—his whole attitude one of menace.

"Furthermore," pursued Bellew placidly, settling the tobacco in his pipe with his thumb, "you can continue to—er demand, until all's blue, and I shall continue to lie here, and smoke, and gaze up at the smiling serenity of heaven."

The black brows of Mr. Cassilis met in a sudden frown, he tossed his whip aside, and took a sudden quick stride towards the recumbent Bellew with so evident an intention, that Small Porges shrank instinctively further within the encircling arm.

But, at that psychic moment, very fortunately for all conc-erned, there came the sound of a quick, light step, and Anthea stood between them.

"Mr. Cassilis!—Mr. Bellew!" she exclaimed, her cheeks flushed, and her bosom heaving with the haste she had made, "pray whatever does this mean?"

Bellew rose to his feet, and seeing Cassilis was silent, shook his head and smiled:

"Upon my word, I hardly know, Miss Anthea. Our friend Mr. Cassilis seems to have got himself all worked up over the—er—sale, I fancy—"

"The furniture!" exclaimed Anthea, and stamped her foot with vexation. "That wretched furniture! Of course you explained your object in buying it, Mr. Bellew?"

"Well, no,—we hadn't got as far as that."

Now when he said this, Anthea's eyes flashed sudden scorn at him, and she curled her lip at him, and turned her back upon him:

"Mr. Bellew bought my furniture because he intends to set up house-keeping—he is to be married—soon, I believe."

"When the moon is at the full!" nodded Bellew.

"Married!" exclaimed Mr. Cassilis, his frown vanishing as if by magic. "Oh, indeed—"

"I am on my way to the hop-gardens, if you care to walk with me, Mr. Cassilis?" and, with the words, Anthea turned, and, as he watched them walk away, together,—Bellew noticed upon the face of Mr. Cassilis an expression very like triumph, and, in his general air, a suggestion of proprietorship that jarred upon him most unpleasantly.

"Why do you frown so, Uncle Porges?"

"I—er—was thinking, nephew."

"Well, I'm thinking, too!" nodded Small Porges, his brows knitted portentously. And thus they sat, Big, and Little Porges, frowning in unison at space for quite a while.

"Are you quite sure you never told my Auntie Anthea that you were going to marry her?" enquired Small Porges, at last.

"Quite sure, comrade,—why?"

"Then how did she know you were going to marry her, an' settle down?"

"Marry—her, and settle down?"

"Yes,—at the full o' the moon, you know."

"Why really—I don't know, my Porges,—unless she guessed it."

"I specks she did,—she's awful' clever at guessing things! But, do you know—"

"Well?"

"I'm thinking I don't just like the way she smiled at Mr. Cassilis, I never saw her look at him like that before,—as if she were awful' glad to see him, you know; so I don't think I'd wait till the full o' the moon, if I were you. I think you'd better marry her—this afternoon."

"That," said Bellew, clapping him on the shoulder, "is a very admirable idea,—I'll mention it to her on the first available opportunity, my Porges."

But the opportunity did not come that day, nor the next, nor the next after that, for it seemed that with the approach of the "Hop-picking" Anthea had no thought, or time, for anything else.

Wherefore Bellew smoked many pipes, and, as the days wore on, possessed his soul in patience, which is a most excellent precept to follow—in all things but love.

CHAPTER XX

Which relates a most extraordinary conversation

In the days which now ensued, while Anthea was busied out of doors and Miss Priscilla was busied indoors, and Small Porges was diligently occupied with his lessons,—at such times, Bellew would take his pipe and go to sit and smoke in company with the Cavalier in the great picture above the carved chimney-piece.

A right jovial companion, at all times, was this Cavalier, an optimist he, from the curling feather in his broad-brimmed beaver hat, to the spurs at his heels. Handsome, gay, and debonair was he, with lips up-curving to a smile beneath his moustachio, and a quizzical light in his grey eyes, very like that in Bellew's own. Moreover he wore the knowing, waggish air of one well versed in all the ways of the world, and mankind in general, and, (what is infinitely more),—of the Sex Feminine, in particular. Experienced was he, beyond all doubt, in their pretty tricks, and foibles, since he had ever been a diligent student of Feminine Capriciousness when the "Merry Monarch" ruled the land.

Hence, it became customary for Bellew to sit with him, and smoke, and take counsel of this "preux chevalier" upon the unfortunate turn of affairs. Whereof ensued many remarkable conversations of which the following, was one:

BELLEW: No sir,—emphatically I do not agree with you. To

be sure, you may have had more experience than I, in such affairs,—but then, it was such a very long time ago.

THE CAVALIER: (Interrupting, or seeming to)!!!

BELLEW: Again, I beg to differ from you, women are not the same to-day as they ever were. Judging by what I have read of the ladies of your day, and King Charles's court at Whitehall,—I should say—not. At least, if they are, they act differently, and consequently must be—er—wooed differently. The methods employed in your day would be wholly inadequate and quite out of place, in this.

THE CAVALIER: (Shaking his head and smirking,—or seeming to)!!!

BELLEW: Well, I'm willing to bet you anything you like that if you were to step down out of your frame, change your velvets and laces for trousers and coat, leave off your great peruke, and wear a derby hat instead of that picturesque, floppy affair, and try your fortune with some Twentieth Century damsel, your high-sounding gallantries, and flattering phrases, would fall singularly flat, and you would be promptly—turned down, sir.

THE CAVALIER: (Tossing his love-locks,—or seeming to)!!!

BELLEW: The "strong hand," you say? Hum! History tells us that William the Conqueror wooed his lady with a club, or a battle-axe, or something of the sort, and she consequently liked him the better for it; which was all very natural, and proper of course, in her case, seeing that hers was the day of battle-axes, and things. But then, as I said before, sir,—the times are sadly changed,—women may still admire strength of body, and even—occasionally—of mind, but the theory of "Dog, woman, and walnut tree" is quite obsolete.

THE CAVALIER: (Frowning and shaking his head,—or seeming to)!!!

BELLEW: Ha!—you don't believe me? Well, that is because you are obsolete, too;—yes sir, as obsolete as your hat, or your boots, or your long rapier. Now, for instance, suppose I were to ask your advice in my own case? You know precisely how the matter stands at present, between Miss Anthea and myself. You also know Miss Anthea personally, since you have seen her much and often, and have watched her grow from childhood into—er—glorious womanhood,—I repeat sir glorious womanhood. Thus, you ought to know, and understand her far better than I,—for I do confess she is a constant source of bewilderment to me. Now, since you do know her so well,—what course should you adopt, were you in my place?

THE CAVALIER: (Smirking more knowingly than ever,—or seeming to)!!!

BELLEW: Preposterous! Quite absurd!—and just what I might have expected. Carry her off, indeed! No no, we are not living in your bad, old, glorious days when a maid's "No" was generally taken to mean "Yes"—or when a lover might swing his reluctant mistress up to his saddle-bow, and ride off with her, leaving the world far behind. To-day it is all changed,—sadly changed. Your age was a wild age, a violent age, but in some respects, perhaps, a rather glorious age. Your advice is singularly characteristic, and, of course, quite impossible, alas!—Carry her off, indeed!

Hereupon, Bellew sighed, and turning away, lighted his pipe, which had gone out, and buried himself in the newspaper.

CHAPTER XXI

Of shoes, and ships, and sealing wax, and the
third finger of the left hand

So Bellew took up the paper. The house was very quiet, for Small Porges was deep in the vexatious rules of the Multiplication Table, and something he called "Jogafrey," Anthea was out, as usual, and Miss Priscilla was busied with her numerous household duties. Thus the brooding silence was unbroken save for the occasional murmur of a voice, the jingle of the housekeeping keys, and the quick, light tap, tap, of Miss Priscilla's stick.

Therefore, Bellew read the paper, and let it be understood that he regarded the daily news-sheet as the last resource of the utterly bored.

Now presently, as he glanced over the paper with a negative interest his eye was attracted by a long paragraph beginning:

At St. George's, Hanover Square, by the Right Reverend the Bishop of—, Silvia Cecile Marchmont, to His Grace the Duke of Ryde, K.G., K.C.B.

Below followed a full, true, and particular account of the ceremony which, it seemed, had been graced by Royalty. George Bellew read it half way through, and—yawned, —positively, and actually, yawned, and thereafter, laughed.

"And so, I have been in Arcadia—only three weeks! I have known Anthea only twenty-one days! A ridiculously short time, as time goes,—in any other place but Arcadia,—and yet sufficient to lay for ever, the—er—Haunting Spectre of the Might Have Been. Lord! what a preposterous ass I was! Baxter was quite right,—utterly, and completely right! Now, let us suppose that this paragraph had read: 'To-day, at St. George's, Hanover Square, Anthea Devine to—' No no,—confound it!" and Bellew crumpled up the paper, and tossed it into a distant corner. "I wonder what Baxter would think of me now,—good old faithful John. The Haunting Spectre of the Might Have Been,—What a preposterous ass!—what a monumental idiot I was!"

"Posterous ass, isn't a very pretty word, Uncle Porges,—or continental idiot!" said a voice behind him, and turning, he beheld Small Porges somewhat stained, and bespattered with ink, who shook a reproving head at him.

"True, nephew," he answered, "but they are sometimes very apt, and in this instance, particularly so."

Small Porges drew near, and, seating himself upon the arm of Bellew's chair, looked at his adopted uncle, long, and steadfastly.

"Uncle Porges," said he, at last, "you never tell stories, do you?—I mean—lies, you know."

"Indeed, I hope not, Porges,—why do you ask?"

"Well,—'cause my Auntie Anthea's 'fraid you do."

"Is she—hum!—Why?"

"When she came to 'tuck me up,' last night, she sat down on my bed, an' talked to me a long time. An' she sighed a lot, an' said she was 'fraid I didn't care for her any more,—which was awful' silly, you know."

"Yes, of course!" nodded Bellew.

"An' then she asked me why I was so fond of you, an' I said 'cause you were my Uncle Porges that I found under a hedge. An' then she got more angrier than ever, an' said she wished I'd left you under the hedge—"

"Did she, my Porges?"

"Yes; she said she wished she'd never seen you, an' she'd be awful' glad when you'd gone away. So I told her you weren't ever going away, an' that we were waiting for the Money Moon to come, an' bring us the fortune. An' then she shook her head, an' said 'Oh! my dear,—you mustn't believe anything he says to you about the moon, or anything else, 'cause he tells lies,'—an' she said 'lies' twice!"

"Ah!—and—did she stamp her foot, Porges?"

"Yes, I think she did; an' then she said there wasn't such a thing as a Money Moon, an' she told me you were going away very soon, to get married, you know."

"And what did you say?"

"Oh! I told her that I was going too. An' then I thought she was going to cry, an' she said 'Oh Georgy! I didn't think you'd leave me—even for him.' So then I had to s'plain how we had arranged that she was going to marry you so that we could all live happy ever after,—I mean, that it was all settled, you know, an' that you were going to speak to her on the first—opportunity. An' then she looked at me a long time an' asked me—was I sure you had said so. An' then she got awful' angry indeed, an' said 'How dare he! Oh, how dare he!' So a course, I told her you'd dare anything—even a dragon,—'cause you are so big, an' brave, you know. So then she went an' stood at the window, an' she was so angry she cried,—an' I nearly cried too. But at last she kissed me 'Good night' an' said you were a man that never meant anything you said, an' that I must never believe you any more, an' that you were going away to marry a lady in London, an' that she was very glad, 'cause then we should all be happy again she s'posed. So she kissed me again, an' tucked me up, an' went away. But it was a long, long time before I could go to sleep, 'cause I kept on thinking, an' thinking s'posing there really wasn't any Money Moon, after all! s'posing you were going to marry another lady in London!—You see, it would all be so—frightfully awful, wouldn't it?"

"Terribly dreadfully awful, my Porges."

"But you never *do* tell lies,—do you, Uncle Porges?"

"No!"

"An'—there *is* a Money Moon, isn't there?"

"Why of course there is."

"An' you *are* going to marry my Auntie Anthea in the full o' the moon, aren't you?"

"Yes, my Porges."

"Why then—everything's all right again,—so let's go an' sit under the hay-stack, an' talk 'bout ships."

"But why of ships?" enquired Bellew, rising.

"Cause I made up my mind, this morning, that I'd be a sailor when I grow up,—a mariner, you know, like Peterday, only I'd prefer to have both my legs."

"You'd find it more convenient, perhaps."

"You know all 'bout oceans, an' waves, and billows, don't you Uncle Porges?"

"Well, I know a little."

"An' are you ever sea-sick,—like a 'landlubber?'"

"I used to be, but I got over it."

"Was it a very big ship that you came over in?"

"No,—not so very big, but she's about as fast as anything in her class, and a corking sea-boat."

"What's her name?"

"Her name?" repeated Bellew, "well, she was called the—er 'Silvia.'"

"That's an awful' pretty name for a ship."

"Hum!—so so,—but I have learned a prettier, and next time she puts out to sea we'll change her name, eh, my Porges?"

"We?" cried Small Porges, looking up with eager eyes, "do you mean you'd take me to sea with you,—an' my Auntie Anthea, of course?"

"You don't suppose I'd leave either of you behind, if I could help it, do you? We'd all sail away together—wherever you wished."

"Do you mean," said Small Porges, in a suddenly awed voice, "that it is—your ship,—your very own?"

"Oh yes-"

"But,—do you know, Uncle Porges, you don't look as though you had a ship—for your very own, somehow."

"Don't I?"

"You see, a ship is such a very big thing for one man to have for his very own self. An' has it got masts, an' funnels, an' anchors?"

"Lots of 'em."

"Then, please, when will you take me an' Auntie Anthea sailing all over the oceans?"

"Just so soon as she is ready to come."

"Then I think I'd like to go to Nova Zembla first,—I found it in my jogafrey to-day, an' it sounds nice an' far off, doesn't it?"

"It does, Shipmate!" nodded Bellew.

"Oh! that's fine!" exclaimed Small Porges rapturously, "you shall be the captain, an' I'll be the shipmate, an' we'll say Aye Aye, to each other—like the real sailors do in books,—shall we?"

"Aye, aye Shipmate!" nodded Bellew again.

"Then please, Uncle Por—I mean Captain,—what shall we name our ship,—I mean the new name?"

"Well, my Porges,—I mean, of course, shipmate,—I rather thought of calling her—Hallo!—why here's the Sergeant."

Sure enough, there was Sergeant Appleby sitting under the shade of "King Arthur"—but who rose, and stood at attention as they came up.

"Why Sergeant, how are you?" said Bellew, gripping the veteran's hand. "You are half an hour before your usual time, to-day,—nothing wrong, I hope?"

"Nothing wrong, Mr. Bellew, sir—I thank you. No, nothing wrong, but this—is a—memorable occasion, sir. May I trouble you to—step behind the tree with me—for half a moment, sir?"

Suiting the action to the word, the Sergeant led Bellew to the other side of the tree, and there, screened from view of the house, he, with a sudden, jerky movement, produced a very small leather case from his pocket, which he handed to Bellew.

"Not good enough—for such a woman—I know, but the best I could afford, sir!" said the Sergeant appearing profoundly interested in the leaves overhead, while Bellew opened the very small box.

"Why—it's very handsome, Sergeant!" said Bellew, making the jewels sparkle in the sun,—"anyone might be proud of such a ring."

"Why, it did look pretty tidy—in the shop, sir,—to me, and Peterday. My comrade has a sharp eye, and a sound judgment in most things, sir—and we took—a deal of trouble in selecting it. But now—when it comes to—giving it to *Her*, —why it looks—uncommon small, and mean, sir."

"A ruby, and two diamonds, and very fine stones, too, Sergeant!"

"So I made so bold as to—come here sir," pursued the Sergeant still interested in the foliage above, "half an hour afore my usual time—to ask you, sir—if you would so far oblige me—as to—hand it to her—when I'm gone, sir."

"Lord, no!" said Bellew, smiling and shaking his head, "not on your life, Sergeant! Why man it would lose half its value in her eyes if any other than you gave it to her. No Sergeant, you must hand it to her yourself, and, what's more, you must slip it upon her finger."

"Good Lord! sir!" exclaimed the Sergeant, "I could never do that!"

"Oh yes you could!"

"Not unless you—stood by me—a force in reserve, as it were, sir."

"I'll do that willingly, Sergeant."

"Then—p 'raps sir—you might happen to know—which finger?"

"The third finger of the left hand, I believe Sergeant."

"Here's Aunt Priscilla now," said Small Porges, at this juncture.

"Lord!" exclaimed the Sergeant, "and sixteen minutes afore her usual time!"

Yes,—there was Miss Priscilla, her basket of sewing upon her arm, as gentle, as unruffled, as placid as usual. And yet it is probable that she divined something from their very attitudes, for there was a light in her eyes, and her cheeks seemed more delicately pink than was their wont. Thus, as she came toward them, under the ancient apple-trees, despite her stick, and her white hair, she looked even younger, and more girlish than ever.

At least, the Sergeant seemed to think so, for, as he met her look, his face grew suddenly radiant, while a slow flush crept up under the tan of his cheek, and the solitary hand he held out to her, trembled a little, for all its size, and strength.

"Miss Priscilla, mam—" he said, and stopped. "Miss Priscilla," he began again, and paused once more.

"Why—Sergeant!" she exclaimed, though it was a very soft little exclamation indeed,—for her hand still rested in his, and so she could feel the quiver of the strong fingers, "why—Sergeant!"

"Miss Priscilla,—" said he, beginning all over again, but with no better success.

"Goodness me!" exclaimed Miss Priscilla, "I do believe he is going to forget to enquire about the peaches!"

"Peaches!" repeated the Sergeant, "Yes, Priscilla."

"And—why?"

"Cause he's brought you a ring," Small Porges broke in, "a very handsome ring, you know, Aunt Priscilla,—all diamonds an' jewels, an' he wants you to please let him put it on your finger—if you don't mind."

"And—here it is!" said the Sergeant, and gave it into her hand.

Miss Priscilla stood very silent, and very still, looking down at the glittering gems, then, all at once, her eyes filled, and a slow wave of colour dyed her cheeks:

"Oh Sergeant!" she said, very softly, "Oh Sergeant, I am only a poor, old woman—with a lame foot!"

"And I am a poor, old soldier—with only one arm, Priscilla."

"You are the strongest, and gentlest, and bravest soldier in all the world, I think!" she answered.

"And you, Priscilla, are the sweetest, and most beautiful *woman* in the world, I *know!* And so—I've loved you all these years, and—never dared to tell you so, because of my—one arm."

"Why then," said Miss Priscilla, smiling up at him through her tears, "if you do—really—think that,—why,—it's this finger, Sergeant!"

So the Sergeant, very clumsily, perhaps, because he had but the one hand, slipped the ring upon the finger in question. And Porges, Big, and Small, turning to glance back, as they went upon their way saw that he still held that small white hand pressed close to his lips.

CHAPTER XXII

Coming events cast their shadows before

"I s'pose they'll be marrying each other, one of these fine days!" said Small Porges as they crossed the meadow, side by side.

"Yes, I expect so, Shipmate," nodded Bellew, "and may they live long, and die happy, say I."

"Aye, aye, Captain,—an' Amen!" returned Small Porges.

Now as they went, conversing of marriage, and ships, and the wonders, and marvels of foreign lands,—they met with Adam who stared up at the sky and muttered to himself, and frowned, and shook his head.

"Good arternoon, Mr. Belloo sir,—an' Master Georgy!"

"Well, Adam, how are the hops?"

"Ops sir,—there never was such 'ops,—no, not in all Kent, sir. All I'm wishin' is that they was all safe picked, an' gathered. W'ot do you make o' them clouds, sir,—over there,—jest over the p'int o' the oast-house?"

Bellew turned, and cast a comprehensive, sailor-like glance in the direction indicated.

"Rain, Adam, and wind,—and plenty of it!" said he.

"Ah! so I think, sir,—driving storm, and thrashing tempest!"

"Well, Adam?"

"Well, sir,—p'raps you've never seen w'ot driving rain, an' raging wind, can do among the 'op-bines, sir. All I wish is that they 'ops was all safe picked an' gathered, sir!" And Adam strode off with his eye still turned heaven-ward, and shaking his head like some great bird of ill-omen.

So the afternoon wore away to evening, and with evening, came Anthea; but a very grave-eyed, troubled Anthea, who sat at the tea-table silent, and preoccupied,—in so much, that Small Porges openly wondered, while Miss Priscilla watched over her, wistful, and tender.

Thus, Tea, which was wont to be the merriest meal of the day, was but the pale ghost of what it should have been, despite Small Porges' flow of conversation, (when not impeded by bread and jam), and Bellew's tactful efforts. Now while he talked light-heartedly, keeping carefully to generalities, he noticed two things,—one was that Anthea made but a pretence at eating, and the second, that though she uttered a word, now and then, yet her eyes persistently avoided his.

Thus, he, for one, was relieved when tea was over, and, as he rose from the table, he determined, despite the unpropitious look of things, to end the suspense, one way or another, and speak to Anthea just so soon as she should be alone.

But here again he was balked and disappointed, for when Small Porges came to bid him good-night as usual, he learned that "Auntie Anthea" had already gone to bed.

"She says it's a head-ache," said Small Porges, "but I 'specks it's the hops, really, you know."

"The hops, my Porges?"

"She's worrying about them,—she's 'fraid of a storm, like Adam is. An' when she worries,—I worry. Oh Uncle Porges!— if only my prayers can bring the Money Moon—soon, you know,—very soon! If they don't bring it in a day or two, —'fraid I shall wake up, one fine morning, an' find I've worried, an' worried myself into an old man."

"Never fear, Shipmate!" said Bellew in his most nautical manner, "'all's well that ends well,'—a-low, and aloft all's a-taunto. So just take a turn at the lee braces, and keep your weather eye lifting, for you may be sure of this,—if the storm does come,—it will bring the Money Moon with it."

Then, having bidden Small Porges a cheery "Good-night"— Bellew went out to walk among the roses. And, as he walked, he watched the flying wrack of clouds above his head, and listened to the wind that moaned in fitful gusts. Wherefore, having learned in his many travels to read, and interpret such natural signs and omens, he shook his head, and muttered to himself—even as Adam had done before him.

Presently he wandered back into the house, and, filling his pipe, went to hold communion with his friend—the Cavalier.

And thus it was that having ensconced himself in the great elbow-chair, and raised his eyes to the picture, he espied a letter tucked into the frame, thereof. Looking closer, he saw that it was directed to himself. He took it down, and, after a momentary hesitation, broke the seal, and read:

Miss Devine presents her compliments to Mr. Bellew, and regrets to say that owing to unforeseen circumstances, she begs that he will provide himself with other quarters at the expiration of the month, being the Twenty-third inst.

Bellew read the lines slowly, twice over, then, folding the note very carefully, put it into his pocket, and stood for a long time staring at nothing in particular. At length he lifted his head, and looked up into the smiling eyes of the Cavalier, above the mantel.

"Sir," said he, very gravely, "it would almost seem that you were in the right of it,—that yours is the best method, after all!" Then he knocked the ashes from his pipe, and went, slowly, and heavily, up-stairs to bed.

It was a long time before he fell asleep, but he did so at last, for Insomnia is a demon who rarely finds his way into Arcadia. But, all at once, he was awake again,—broad awake, and staring into the dark, for a thousand voices seemed to be screaming in his ears, and eager hands were shaking, and plucking at window and lattice. He started up, and then he knew that the storm was upon them, at last, in all its fury, —rain, and a mighty wind,—a howling raging tempest. Yes, a great, and mighty wind was abroad,—it shrieked under the eaves, it boomed and bellowed in the chimneys, and roared away to carry destruction among the distant woods; while the rain beat hissing against the window-panes.

Surely in all its many years the old house of Dapplemere had seldom borne the brunt of such a storm, so wild,—so fierce, and pitiless!

And, lying there upon his bed, listening to the uproar, and tumult, Bellew must needs think of her who had once said:

"We are placing all our hopes, this year, upon the hops!"

CHAPTER XXIII

How Small Porges, in his hour of need, was deserted by his Uncle

"Ruined, sir!—Done for!—Lord love me! they ain't worth the trouble o? gatherin'—w'ot's left on 'em, Mr. Belloo sir."

"So bad as that, Adam?"

"Bad!—ah, so bad as ever was, sir!" said Adam, blinking suspiciously, and turning suddenly away.

"Has Miss Anthea seen,—does she know?"

"Ah! she were out at dawn, and Oh Lord, Mr. Belloo sir! I can't never forget her poor, stricken face,—so pale and sad it were. But she never said nothing, only: 'Oh, Adam!—my poor hops!' An' I see her lips all of a quiver while she spoke. An' so she turned away, an' came back to the 'ouse, sir. Poor lass! Oh poor lass!" he exclaimed, his voice growing more husky. "She's made a brave fight for it, sir,—but it weren't no use, ye see,—it'll be 'Good-bye' for her to Dapplemere, arter all, that there mortgage can't never be paid now,—nohow."

"When is it due?"

"Well, according to the bond, or the deed, or whatever they calls it,—it be doo—tonight, at nine o'clock, sir,—though Old Grimes,—as a special favour, an' arter much persuading,—'ad agreed to hold over till next Saturday,—on account o' the ' op-picking. But now—seeing as there ain't no 'ops to be picked,—why he'll fore-close to-night, an' glad enough to do it, you can lay your oath on that, Mr. Belloo sir."

"To-night!" said Bellew, "to-night!" and he stood, for a while with bent head, as though lost in profound thought. "Adam," said he, suddenly, "help me to harness the mare, I must drive over to the nearest rail-road depot,—hurry, I must be off, the sooner, the better."

"What!—be you—goin' sir?"

"Yes;—hurry, man,—hurry!"

"D'ye mean as you're a-goin' to leave her—now, in the middle o' all this trouble?"

"Yes, Adam,—I must go to London—on business,—now hurry, like a good fellow." And so, together they entered the stable, and together they harnessed the mare. Which done, staying not for breakfast, Bellew mounted the driver's seat, and, with Adam beside him, drove rapidly away.

But Small Porges had seen these preparations, and now came running all eagerness, but ere he could reach the yard, Bellew was out of ear-shot.

So there stood Small Porges, a desolate little figure, watching the rapid course of the dogcart until it had vanished over the brow of the hill. And then, all at once the tears welled up into his eyes hot, and scalding, and a great sob burst from him, for it seemed to him that his beloved Uncle Porges had failed him at the crucial moment,—had left him solitary just when he needed him most.

Thus Small Porges gave way to his grief, hidden in the very darkest corner of the stable, whither he had retired lest any should observe his weakness, until having once more gained command of himself, and wiped away his tears with his small, and dingy pocket-handkerchief, he slowly re-crossed the yard, and entering the house went to look for his Auntie Anthea.

And, after much search, he found her—half-lying, half-kneeling beside his bed. When he spoke to her, though she answered him, she did not look up, and he knew that she was weeping.

"Don't, Auntie Anthea,—don't!" he pleaded. "I know Uncle Porges has gone away, an' left us, but you've got me left, you know,—an' I shall be a man—very soon,—before my time, I think. So—don't cry,—though I'm awful' sorry he's gone, too—just when we needed him the most, you know!"

"Oh Georgy!" she whispered, "my dear, brave little Georgy! We shall only have each other soon,—they're going to take Dapplemere away from us,—and everything we have in the world,—Oh Georgy!"

"Well, never mind!" said he, kneeling beside her, and drawing one small arm protectingly about her, "we shall always have each other left, you know,—nobody shall ever take you away from me. An' then—there's the—Money Moon! It's been an awful' long time coming,—but it may come to-night, or tomorrow night. *He* said it would be sure to come if the storm came, an' so I'll find the fortune for you at last. I know I shall find it *some day* a course—'cause I've prayed, an' prayed for it so very hard, an' *He* said my prayers went straight up to heaven, an' didn't get blown away, or lost in the clouds. So—don't cry, Auntie Anthea let's wait—just a little longer—till the Money Moon comes."

Jeffery Farnol

CHAPTER XXIV

In which shall be found mention of a certain black bag

"Baxter!"

"Sir?"

"Get me a pen, and ink!"

"Yes, sir."

Now any ordinary mortal might have manifested just a little surprise to behold his master walk suddenly in, dusty and dishevelled of person, his habitual languor entirely laid aside, and to thus demand pen and ink, forthwith. But then, Baxter, though mortal, was the very cream of a gentleman's gentleman, and the acme of valets, (as has been said), and comported himself accordingly.

"Baxter!"

"Sir?"

"Oblige me by getting this cashed."

"Yes, sir."

"Bring half of it in gold."

"Sir," said Baxter, glancing down at the slip of paper, "did you say—half, sir?"

"Yes, Baxter,—I'd take it all in gold only that it would be rather awkward to drag around. So bring half in gold, and the rest in—five pound notes."

"Very good, sir!"

"And—Baxter!"

"Sir?"

"Take a cab!"

"Certainly sir." And Baxter went out, closing the door behind him. Meanwhile Bellew busied himself in removing all traces of his journey, and was already bathed, and shaved, and dressed, by the time Baxter returned.

Now gripped in his right hand Baxter carried a black leather bag which jingled as he set it down upon the table.

"Got it?" enquired Bellew.

"I have, sir."

"Good!" nodded Bellew. "Now just run around to the garage, and fetch the new racing car,—the Mercedes."

"Now, sir?"

"Now, Baxter!"

Once more Baxter departed, and, while he was gone, Bellew began to pack,—that is to say, he bundled coats and trousers, shirts and boots into a portmanteau in a way that would have wrung Baxter's heart, could he have seen. Which done, Bellew opened the black bag, glanced inside, shut it again, and, lighting his pipe, stretched himself out upon an ottoman, and immediately became plunged in thought.

So lost was he, indeed, that Baxter, upon his return was necessitated to emit three distinct coughs,—(the most perfectly proper, and gentleman-like coughs in the world) ere Bellew was aware of his presence.

"Oh!—that you, Baxter?" said he, sitting up, "back so soon?"

"The car is at the door, sir."

"The car?—ah yes, to be sure!—Baxter."

"Sir?"

"What should you say if I told you—" Bellew paused to strike a match, broke it, tried another, broke that, and finally put his pipe back into his pocket, very conscious the while of Baxter's steady, though perfectly respectful regard.

"Baxter," said he again.

"Sir?" said Baxter.

"What should you say if I told you that I was in love—at last, Baxter!—Head over ears—hopelessly—irretrievably?"

"Say, sir?—why I should say,—indeed, sir?"

"What should you say," pursued Bellew, staring thoughtfully down at the rug under his feet, "if I told you that I am so very much, in love that I am positively afraid to—tell her so?"

"I should say—very remarkable, sir!"

Bellew took out his pipe again, looked at it very much as if he had never seen such a thing before, and laid it down upon the mantelpiece.

"Baxter," said he, "kindly understand that I am speaking to you as—er—man to man,—as my father's old and trusted servant and my early boy-hood's only friend; sit down, John."

"Thank you, Master George, sir."

"I wish to—confess to you, John, that—er—regarding the—er—Haunting Spectre of the Might Have Been,—you were entirely in the right. At that time I knew no more the meaning of the—er—the word, John—"

"Meaning the word—Love, Master George!"

"Precisely; I knew no more about it than—that table. But during these latter days, I have begun to understand, and—er—the fact of the matter is—I'm—I'm fairly—up against it, John!"

Here, Baxter, who had been watching him with his quick, sharp eyes nodded his head solemnly:

"Master George," said he, "speaking as your father's old servant, and your boyhood's friend,—I'm afraid you are."

Bellew took a turn up and down the room, and then pausing in front of Baxter, (who had risen also, as a matter of course), he suddenly laid his two hands upon his valet's shoulders.

"Baxter," said he, "you'll remember that after my mother died, my father was always too busy piling up his millions to give much time or thought to me, and I should have been a very lonely small boy if it hadn't been for you, John Baxter. I was often 'up against it,' in those days, John, and you were always ready to help, and advise me;—but now,—well, from the look of things, I'm rather afraid that I must stay 'up against it'— that the game is lost already, John. But which ever way Fate decides—win, or lose,—I'm glad—yes, very glad to have learned the true meaning of—the word, John."

"Master George, sir,—there was a poet once—Tennyson, I think, who said,—'Tis better to have loved and lost than never to have loved at all,' and I know—that he was—right. Many years ago,—before you were born, Master George, I loved—and lost, and that is how I know. But I hope that Fortune will be kinder to you, indeed I do."

"Thank you, John,—though I don't see why she should be." And Bellew stood staring down at the rug again, till aroused by Baxter's cough:

"Pray sir, what are your orders, the car is waiting downstairs?"

"Orders?—why—er—pack your grip, Baxter, I shall take you with me, this time, into Arcadia, Baxter."

"For how long, sir?"

"Probably a week."

"Very good, sir."

"It is now half-past three, I must be back in Dapplemere at eight. Take your time—I'll go down to look at the machine. Just lock the place up, and—er—don't forget the black bag."

Some ten minutes later the great racing car set out on its journey, with Bellew at the wheel, and Baxter beside him with the black bag held firmly upon his knee.

Their process was, necessarily, slow at first, on account of the crowded thoroughfares. But, every now and then, the long, low car would shoot forward through some gap in the traffic, grazing the hubs of bus-wheels, dodging hansoms, shaving sudden corners in an apparently reckless manner. But Baxter, with his hand always upon the black leather bag, sat calm and unruffled, since he knew, by long experience, that Bellew's eye was quick and true, and his hand firm and sure upon the wheel.

Over Westminster Bridge, and along the Old Kent Road they sped, now fast, now slow,—threading a tortuous, and difficult way amid the myriad vehicles, and so, betimes, they reached Blackheath.

And now the powerful machine hummed over that ancient road that had aforetime, shaken to the tread of stalwart Roman Legionaries,—up Shooter's Hill, and down,—and so into the open country.

And, ever as they went, they talked. And not as master and servant but as "between man and man,"—wherefore Baxter the Valet became merged and lost in Baxter the Human,—the honest John of the old days,—a gray haired, kindly-eyed, middle-aged cosmopolitan who listened to, and looked at, Young Alcides beside him as if he had indeed been the Master George, of years ago.

"So you see, John, if all things *do* go well with me, we should probably take a trip to the Mediterranean."

"In the—'Silvia,' of course, Master George?"

"Yes; though—er—I've decided to change her name, John."

"Ah!—very natural—under the circumstances, Master George," said honest John, his eyes twinkling slyly as he spoke, "Now, if I might suggest a new name it would be hard to find a more original one than 'The Haunting Spectre of the—"

"Bosh, John!—there never was such a thing, you were quite right, as I said before, and—by heaven,—potato sacks!"

"Eh,—what?—potato sacks, Master George?"

They had been climbing a long, winding ascent, but now, having reached the top of the hill, they overtook a great, lumbering market cart, or wain, piled high with sacks of potatoes, and driven by an extremely surly-faced man in a smock-frock.

"Hallo there!" cried Bellew, slowing up, "how much for one of your potato-sacks?"

"Get out, now!" growled the surly-faced man, in a tone as surly as his look, "can't ye see as they're all occipied?"

"Well,—empty one."

"Get out, now!" repeated the man, scowling blacker than ever.

"I'll give you a sovereign for one."

"Now, don't ye try to come none o' your jokes wi' me, young feller!" growled the carter. "Sovereign!—bah!—Show us."

"Here it is," said Bellew, holding up the coin in question. "Catch!" and, with the word, he tossed it up to the carter who caught it, very dexterously, looked at it, bit it, rubbed it on his sleeve, rang it upon the foot-board of his waggon, bit it again and finally pocketed it.

"It's a go, sir," he nodded, his scowl vanishing as by magic; and as he spoke, he turned, seized the nearest sack, and, forthwith sent a cascade of potatoes rolling, and bounding all over the road. Which done, he folded up the sack, and handed it down to Bellew who thrust it under the seat, nodded, and, throwing in the clutch, set off down the road. But, long after the car had hummed itself out of sight, and the dust of its going had subsided, the carter sat staring after it—open-mouthed.

If Baxter wondered at this purchase, he said nothing, only he bent his gaze thoughtfully upon the black leather bag that he held upon his knee.

On they sped between fragrant hedges, under whispering trees, past lonely cottages and farm-houses, past gate, and field, and wood, until the sun grew low.

At last, Bellew stopped the automobile at a place where a narrow lane, or cart track, branched off from the high road, and wound away between great trees.

"I leave you here," said he as he sprang from the car, "this is Dapplemere,—the farmhouse lies over the up-land, yonder, though you can't see it because of the trees."

"Is it far, Master George?"

"About half a mile."

"Here is the bag, sir; but—do you think it is—quite safe—?"

"Safe, John?"

"Under the circumstances, Master George, I think it would be advisable to—to take this with you." And he held out a small revolver. Bellew laughed, and shook his head.

"Such things aren't necessary—here in Arcadia, John,—besides, I have my stick. So good-bye, for the present, you'll stay at the 'King's Head,'—remember."

"Good-night, Master George, sir, goodnight! and good fortune go with you."

"Thank you!" said Bellew, and reached out his hand, "I think we'll shake on that, John!"

So they clasped hands, and Bellew turned, and set off along the grassy lane. And, presently, as he went, he heard the hum of the car grow rapidly fainter and fainter until it was lost in the quiet of the evening.

CHAPTER XXV

The Conspirators

The shadows were creeping down, and evening was approaching, as Bellew took his way along that winding lane that led to the House of Dapplemere.

Had there been anyone to see, (which there was not), they might have noticed something almost furtive in his manner of approach, for he walked always under the trees where the shadows lay thickest, and paused, once or twice, to look about him warily. Being come within sight of the house, he turned aside, and forcing his way through a gap in the hedge, came by a roundabout course to the farm-yard. Here, after some search, he discovered a spade, the which, (having discarded his stick), he took upon his shoulder, and with the black leather bag tucked under his arm, crossed the paddock with the same degree of caution, and so, at last, reached the orchard. On he went, always in the shadow until, at length, he paused beneath the mighty, knotted branches of "King Arthur." Never did conspirator glance about him with sharper eyes, or hearken with keener ears, than did George Bellew,—or Conspirator No. One, where he now stood beneath the protecting shadow of "King Arthur,"—or Conspirator No. Two, as, having unfolded the potato sack, he opened the black leather bag.

The moon was rising broad, and yellow, but it was low as yet, and "King Arthur" stood in impenetrable gloom,—as any other thorough-going, self-respecting conspirator should; and now, all at once, from this particular patch of shadow, there came a sudden sound,—a rushing sound,—a chinking, clinking, metallic sound, and, thereafter, a crisp rustling that was not the rustling of ordinary paper.

And now Conspirator No. One rises, and ties the mouth of the sack with string he had brought with him for the purpose, and setting down the sack, bulky now and heavy, by Conspirator No. Two, takes up the spade and begins to dig. And, in a while, having made an excavation not very deep to be sure, but sufficient to his purpose, he deposits the sack within, covers it with soil, treads it down, and replacing the torn sod, carefully pats it down with the flat of his spade. Which thing accomplished, Conspirator No. One wipes his brow, and stepping forth of the shadow, consults his watch with anxious eye, and, thereupon, smiles,—surely a singularly pleasing smile for the lips of an arch-conspirator to wear. Thereafter he takes up the black bag, empty now, shoulders the spade, and sets off, keeping once more in the shadows, leaving Conspirator No. Two to guard their guilty secret.

Now, as Conspirator No. One goes his shady way, he keeps his look directed towards the rising moon, and thus he almost runs into one who also stands amid the shadows and whose gaze is likewise fixed upon the moon.

"Ah?—Mr. Bellew!" exclaims a drawling voice, and Squire Cassilis turns to regard him with his usual supercilious smile. Indeed Squire Cassilis seems to be even more self-satisfied, and smiling than ordinary, to-night,—or at least Bellew imagines so.

"You are still agriculturally inclined, I see," said Mr. Cassilis, nodding towards the spade, "though it's rather a queer time to choose for digging, isn't it?"

"Not at all, sir—not at all," returned Bellew solemnly, "the moon is very nearly at the full, you will perceive."

"Well, sir,—and what of that?"

"When the moon is at the full, or nearly so, I generally dig, sir,—that is to say, circumstances permitting."

"Really," said Mr. Cassilis beginning to caress his moustache, "it seems to me that you have very—ah—peculiar tastes, Mr. Bellew."

"That is because you have probably never experienced the fierce joys of moon-light digging, sir."

"No, Mr. Bellew,—digging—as a recreation, has never appealed to me at any time."

"Then sir," said Bellew, shaking his head, "permit me to tell you that you have missed a great deal. Had I the time, I should be delighted to explain to you exactly how much, as it is— allow me to wish you a very good evening."

Mr. Cassilis smiled, and his teeth seemed to gleam whiter, and sharper than ever in the moon-light:

"Wouldn't it be rather more apropos if you said—'Good-bye' Mr. Bellew?" he enquired. "You are leaving Dapplemere, shortly, I understand,—aren't you?"

"Why sir," returned Bellew, grave, and imperturbable as ever,—"it all depends."

"Depends!—upon what, may I ask?"

"The moon, sir."

"The moon?"

"Precisely!"

"And pray—what can the moon have to do with

your departure?"

"A great deal more than you'd think—sir. Had I the time, I should be delighted to explain to you exactly how much, as it is,—permit me to wish you a very—good evening!"

Saying which, Bellew nodded affably, and, shouldering his spade, went upon his way. And still he walked in the shadows, and still he gazed upon the moon, but now, his thick brows were gathered in a frown, and he was wondering just why Cassilis should chance to be here, to-night, and what his confident air, and the general assurance of his manner might portend; above all, he was wondering how Mr. Cassilis came to be aware of his own impending departure. And so, at last, he came to the rick-yard,—full of increasing doubt and misgivings.

CHAPTER XXVI

How the money moon rose

Evening had deepened into night,—a night of ineffable calm, a night of an all pervading quietude. A horse snorted in the stable nearby, a dog barked in the distance, but these sounds served only to render the silence the more profound, by contrast. It was, indeed, a night wherein pixies, and elves, and goblins, and fairies might weave their magic spells, a night wherein tired humanity dreamed those dreams that seem so hopelessly impossible by day.

And, over all, the moon rose high, and higher, in solemn majesty, filling the world with her pale loveliness, and brooding over it like the gentle goddess she is. Even the distant dog seemed to feel something of all this, for, after a futile bark or two, he gave it up altogether, and was heard no more.

And Bellew, gazing up at Luna's pale serenity, smiled and nodded,—as much as to say, "You'll do!" and so stood leaning upon his spade listening to:

> "That deep hush which seems a sigh
> Breathed by Earth to listening sky."

Now, all at once, upon this quietude there rose a voice up-raised in fervent supplication; wherefore, treading very softly, Bellew came, and peeping round the hay-rick, beheld Small Porges upon his knees. He was equipped for travel and the perils of the road, for beside him lay a stick, and tied to this stick was a bundle that bulged with his most cherished possessions. His cheeks were wet with great tears that glistened in the moon-beams, but he wept with eyes tight shut, and with his small hands clasped close together, and thus he spoke, —albeit much shaken, and hindered by sobs:

"I s'pose you think I bother you an awful lot, dear Lord,—an' so I do, but you haven't sent the Money Moon yet, you see, an' now my Auntie Anthea's got to leave Dapplemere—if I don't find the fortune for her soon. I know I'm crying a lot, an' real men don't cry,—but it's only 'cause I'm awful—lonely an' disappointed,—an' nobody can see me, so it doesn't matter. But, dear Lord, I've looked an' looked everywhere, an' I haven't found a single sovereign yet,—an' I've prayed to you, an' prayed to you for the Money Moon an'—it's never come. So now, dear Lord, I'm going to Africa, an' I want you to please take care of my Auntie Anthea till I come back. Sometimes I'm 'fraid my prayers can't quite manage to get up to you 'cause of the clouds, an' wind, but to-night there isn't any, so, if they do reach you, please—Oh! please let me find the fortune, and, if you don't mind, let—*him* come back to me, dear Lord,—I mean my Uncle Porges, you know. An' now—that's all, dear Lord, so Amen!"

As the prayer ended Bellew stole back, and coming to the gate of the rick-yard, leaned there waiting. And, presently, as he watched, he saw a small figure emerge from behind the big hay-stack and come striding manfully toward him, his bundle upon his shoulder, and with the moon bright in his curls.

But, all at once, Small Porges saw him and stopped, and the stick and bundle fell to the ground and lay neglected.

"Why—my Porges!" said Bellew, a trifle huskily, perhaps, "why, Shipmate!" and he held out his hands. Then Small Porges uttered a cry, and came running, and next moment Big Porges had him in his arms.

Jeffery Farnol

"Oh, Uncle Porges!—then you—have come back to me!"

"Aye, aye, Shipmate."

"Why, then—my prayers *did* reach!"

"Why, of course,—prayers always reach, my Porges."

"Then, oh!—do you s'pose I shall find the fortune, too?"

"Not a doubt of it,—just look at the moon!"

"The—moon?"

"Why, haven't you noticed how—er—peculiar it is to-night?"

"Peculiar?" repeated Small Porges breathlessly, turning to look at it.

"Why, yes, my Porges,—big, you know, and—er—yellow, —like—er—like a very large sovereign."

"Do you mean—Oh! do you mean—it's—the—" But here Small Porges choked suddenly, and could only look his question.

"The Money Moon?—Oh yes—there she is at last, my Porges! Take a good look at her, I don't suppose we shall ever see another."

Small Porges stood very still, and gazed up at the moon's broad, yellow disc, and, as he looked the tears welled up in his eyes again, and a great sob broke from him.

"I'm so—glad!" he whispered. "So—awful—glad!" Then, suddenly, he dashed away his tears and slipped his small, trembling hand into Bellew's.

"Quick, Uncle Porges!" said he, "Mr. Grimes is coming

to-night, you know—an' we must find the money in time. Where shall we look first?"

"Well, I guess the orchard will do—to start with."

"Then let's go—now."

"But we shall need a couple of spades, Shipmate."

"Oh!—must we dig?"

"Yes,—I fancy that's a—er—digging moon, my Porges, from the look of it. Ah! there's a spade, nice and handy, you take that and I'll—er—I'll manage with this pitchfork."

"But you can't dig with a—"

"Oh! well—you can do the digging, and I'll just—er—prod, you know. Ready?—then heave ahead, Shipmate."

So they set out, hand in hand, spade and pitch-fork on shoulder, and presently were come to the orchard.

"It's an awful big place to dig up a fortune in!" said Small Porges, glancing about. "Where do you s'pose we'd better begin?"

"Well, Shipmate, between you and me, and the pitch-fork here, I rather fancy 'King Arthur' knows more than most people would think. Any way, we'll try him. You dig on that side, and I'll prod on this."

Saying which, Bellew pointed to a certain spot where the grass looked somewhat uneven, and peculiarly bumpy, and, bidding Small Porges get to work, went round to the other side of the great tree.

Being there, he took out his pipe, purely from force of habit, and stood with it clenched in his teeth, listening to the scrape of Small Porges' spade.

Presently he heard a cry, a panting, breathless cry, but full of a joy unspeakable:

"I've got it!—Oh, Uncle Porges—I've found it!"

Small Porges was down upon his knees, pulling and tugging at a sack he had partially unearthed, and which, with Bellew's aid, he dragged forth into the moonlight. In the twinkling of an eye the string was cut, and plunging in a hand Small Porges brought up a fistful of shining sovereigns, and, among them, a crumpled banknote.

"It's all right, Uncle Porges!" he nodded, his voice all of a quaver. "It's all right, now,—I've found the fortune I've prayed for,—gold, you know, an' banknotes—in a sack. Everything will be all right again now." And, while he spoke, he rose to his feet, and lifting the sack with an effort, swung it across his shoulder, and set off toward the house.

"Is it heavy, Shipmate?"

"Awful heavy!" he panted, "but I don't mind that—it's gold, you see!" But, as they crossed the rose-garden, Bellew laid a restraining hand upon his shoulder.

"Porges," said he, "where is your Auntie Anthea?"

"In the drawing-room, waiting for Mr. Grimes."

"Then, come this way." And turning, Bellew led Small Porges up, and along the terrace.

"Now, my Porges," he admonished him, "when we come to the drawing-room windows,—they're open, you see,—I want you to hide with me in the shadows, and wait until I give you the word—"

"Aye, aye, Captain!" panted Small Porges.

"When I say 'heave ahead, Shipmate,'—why, then, you will take your treasure upon your back and march straight into the room—you understand?"

"Aye, aye, Captain."

"Why, then—come on, and—mum's the word."

Very cautiously they approached the long French windows, and paused in the shadow of a great rose-bush, near-by. From where he stood Bellew could see Anthea and Miss Priscilla, and between them, sprawling in an easy chair, was Grimes, while Adam, hat in hand, scowled in the background.

"All I can say is—as I'm very sorry for ye, Miss Anthea," Grimes was saying. "Ah! that I am, but glad as you've took it so well,—no crying nor nonsense!" Here he turned to look at Miss Priscilla, whose everlasting sewing had fallen to her feet, and lay there all unnoticed, while her tearful eyes were fixed upon Anthea, standing white-faced beside her.

"And when—when shall ye be ready to—leave, to—vacate Dapplemere, Miss Anthea?" Grimes went on. "Not as I mean to 'urry you, mind,—only I should like you to—name a day."

Now, as Bellew watched, he saw Anthea's lips move, but no sound came. Miss Priscilla saw also, and catching the nerveless hand, drew it to her bosom, and wept over it.

"Come! come!" expostulated Grimes, jingling the money in his pockets. "Come, come, Miss Anthea, mam!—all as I'm axing you is—when? All as I want you to do is—"

But here Adam, who had been screwing and wringing at his hat, now stepped forward and, tapping Grimes upon the shoulder, pointed to the door:

Jeffery Farnol

"Mister Grimes," said he, "Miss Anthea's told ye all as you come here to find out,—she's told ye as she—can't pay, so now,—s'pose you—go."

"But all I want to know is when she'll be ready to move, and I ain't a going till I do,—so you get out o' my way!"

"S'pose you go!" repeated Adam.

"Get out o' my way,—d'ye hear?"

"Because," Adam went on, "if ye don't go, Mister Grimes, the 'Old Adam' be arising inside o' me to that degree as I shall be forced to ketch you by the collar o' your jacket, and—heave you out, Mr. Grimes, sir,—so s'pose you go."

Hereupon Mr. Grimes rose, put on his hat, and muttering to himself, stamped indignantly from the room, and Adam, shutting the door upon him, turned to Miss Anthea, who stood white-lipped and dry-eyed, while gentle little Miss Priscilla fondled her listless hand.

"Don't,—don't look that way, Miss Anthea," said Adam. "I'd rayther see you cry, than look so. It be 'ard to 'ave to let the old place go, but—"

"Heave ahead, Shipmate!" whispered Bellew.

Obedient to his command Small Porges, with his burden upon his back, ran forward, and stumbled into the room.

"It's all right, Auntie Anthea!" he cried, "I've got the fortune for you,—I've found the money I prayed for,—here it is, oh!—here it is!"

The sack fell jingling to the floor, and, next moment, he had poured a heap of shining gold and crumpled banknotes at Anthea's feet.

For a moment no one moved, then, with a strange hoarse cry, Adam had flung himself down upon his knees, and caught up a great handful of the gold; then while Miss Priscilla sobbed with her arms about Small Porges, and Anthea stared down at the treasure, wide-eyed, and with her hands pressed down upon her heart, Adam gave a sudden, great laugh, and springing up, came running out through the window, never spying Bellew in his haste, and shouting as he ran:

"Grimes!" he roared, "Oh! Grimes, come back an' be paid. Come back—we've had our little joke wi' you,—now come back an' be paid!"

Then, at last, Anthea's stony calm was broken, her bosom heaved with tempestuous sobs, and, next moment, she had thrown herself upon her knees, and had clasped her arms about Small Porges and Aunt Priscilla, mingling kisses with her tears. As for Bellew, he turned away, and, treading a familiar path, found himself beneath the shadow of "King Arthur." Therefore, he sat down, and lighting his pipe, stared up at the glory of the full-orbed moon.

"Happiness," said he, speaking his thought aloud, "Happiness shall come riding astride the full moon!' Now—I wonder!"

CHAPTER XXVII

In which is verified the adage of the cup and the lip.

Now as he sat thus, plunged in thought, he heard the voice of one who approached intoning a familiar chant, or refrain,—the voice was harsh, albeit not unmusical, and the words of the chant were these:

"When I am dead, diddle diddle, as well may hap,
Bury me deep, diddle diddle, under the tap,
Under the tap, diddle diddle, I'll tell you—"

"Lord!" exclaimed the singer, breaking off suddenly, "be that you, Mr. Belloo, sir?"

"Yea, in good sooth, Adam, the very same,—but you sing, Adam?"

"Ah!—I sing, Mr. Belloo, sir, an' if you ax me why, then I tell you because I be 'appy-'earted an' full o' j-o-y, j'y, sir. The mortgage be paid off at last, Mr. Belloo, sir,—Miss Anthea be out o' debt,—free, sir,—an' all along o' Master Georgy, God bless him!"

"Oh!" said Bellew, "—er—that's good!"

"Good!" exclaimed Adam, "Ah, Mr. Belloo sir! it be more than good,—it's saved Miss Anthea's home for her, and—betwixt you an' me, sir,—I think it's saved her too. An' it be all along o' that Master Georgy! Lord sir! many's the time as I've watched that theer blessed b'y a-seekin', an' a-searchin', a pokin' an' a pryin' round the place a-lookin' for 'is fortun', —but, Lord bless my eyes an' limbs, sir!—I never thought as he'd find nothin'."

"Why, of course not, Adam."

"Ah!—but that's jest where I were mistook, Mr. Belloo, sir, —because 'e did."

"Did what, Adam?"

"Found the fortun' as he were always a-lookin' for,—a sack o' golden soverings, sir, an' bank-notes, Mr. Belloo, sir,—bushels on 'em; enough—ah! more 'n enough to pay off that mortgage, and to send that theer old Grimes about his business,—an' away from Dapplemere for good an' all, sir."

"So Grimes is really paid off, then, is he, Adam?"

"I done it myself, sir,—wi' these here two 'ands,—Three thousand pound I counted over to him, an' five hundred more—in banknotes, sir, while Miss Anthea sat by like one in a dream. Altogether there were five thousand pound as that blessed b'y dug up out o' the orchard—done up all in a pertater sack, under this very i-dentical tree as you'm a-set-tin' under Mr. Belloo sir. E'cod, I be half minded to take a shovel and have a try at fortun'-huntin' myself,—only there ain't much chance o' findin' another, hereabouts; besides—that b'y prayed for that fortun', ah! long, an' hard he prayed, Mr. Belloo sir, an'—'twixt you an' me, sir, I ain't been much of a pray-er myself since my old mother died. Anyhow, the mortgage be paid off, sir, Miss Anthea's free, an' 'tis joy'ful, an' 'appy-'earted I be this night. Prudence an' me'll be gettin' married soon now,—an' when I think of her cookin'—Lord, Mr. Belloo sir!—All as I say is God bless Master Georgy! Good-night, sir! an' may your dreams be as 'appy as mine,—always supposin' I do dream, —which is seldom.

Good-night, sir!"

Long after Adam's cheery whistle had died away, Bellew sat, pipe in mouth, staring up at the moon. At length, however, he rose, and turned his steps towards the house.

"Mr. Bellew!"

He started, and turning, saw Anthea standing amid her roses. For a moment they looked upon each other in silence, as though each dreaded to speak, then suddenly, she turned, and broke a great rose from its stem, and stood twisting it between her fingers.

"Why did you—do it?" she asked.

"Do it?" he repeated.

"I mean the—fortune. Georgy told me—how you—helped him to find it, and I—*know* how it came there, of course. Why did you—do it?"

"You didn't tell him—how it came there?" asked Bellew anxiously.

"No," she answered, "I think it would break his heart—if he knew."

"And I think it would have broken his heart if he had never found it," said Bellew, "and I couldn't let that happen, could I?" Anthea did not answer, and he saw that her eyes were very bright in the shadow of her lashes though she kept them lowered to the rose in her fingers.

"Anthea!" said he, suddenly, and reached out his hand to her. But she started and drew from his touch.

"Don't!" she said, speaking almost in a whisper, "don't touch me. Oh! I know you have paid off the mortgage—you have bought back my home for me as you bought back my furniture! Why?—why? I was nothing to you, or you to me, —why have you laid me under this obligation,—you know I can never hope to return your money—oh! why,—why did you do it?"

"Because I—love you, Anthea, have loved you from the first. Because everything I possess in this world is yours—even as I am."

"You forget!" she broke in proudly, "you forget—"

"Everything but my love for you, Anthea,—everything but that I want you for my wife. I'm not much of a fellow, I know, but—could you learn to—love me enough to—marry me— some day, Anthea?"

"Would you have—dared to say this to me—before to-night?—before your money had bought back the roof over my head? Oh! haven't I been humiliated enough? You—you have taken from me the only thing I had left—my independence, —stolen it from me! Oh! hadn't I been shamed enough?"

Now, as she spoke, she saw that his eyes were grown suddenly big and fierce, and, in that moment, her hands were caught in his powerful clasp.

"Let me go!" she cried.

"No," said he, shaking his head, "not until you tell me if you —love me. Speak, Anthea."

"Loose my hands!" She threw up her head proudly, and her eyes gleamed, and her cheeks flamed with sudden anger. "Loose me!" she repeated. But Bellew only shook his head, and his chin seemed rather more prominent than usual, as he answered:

"Tell me that you love me, or that you hate me—whichever it

is, but, until you do—"

"You—hurt me!" said she, and then, as his fingers relaxed, —with a sudden passionate cry, she had broken free; but, even so, he had caught and swept her up in his arms, and held her close against his breast. And now, feeling the hopelessness of further struggle, she lay passive, while her eyes flamed up into his, and his eyes looked down into hers. Her long, thick hair had come loose, and now with a sudden, quick gesture, she drew it across her face, veiling it from him; wherefore, he stooped his head above those lustrous tresses.

"Anthea!" he murmured, and the masterful voice was strangely hesitating, and the masterful arms about her were wonderfully gentle, "Anthea—do you—love me?" Lower he bent, and lower, until his lips touched her hair, until beneath that fragrant veil, his mouth sought, and found, hers, and, in that breathless moment, he felt them quiver responsive to his caress. And then, he had set her down, she was free, and he was looking at her with a new-found radiance in his eyes.

"Anthea!" he said, wonderingly, "why then—you do—?" But, as he spoke, she hid her face in her hands.

"Anthea!" he repeated.

"Oh!" she whispered, "I—hate you!—despise you! Oh! you shall be paid back,—every penny,—every farthing, and—very soon! Next week—I marry Mr. Cassilis!"

And so, she turned, and fled away, and left him standing there amid the roses.

CHAPTER XXVIII

Which tells how Bellew left Dapplemere in the dawn

Far in the East a grey streak marked the advent of another day, and upon all things was a solemn hush, a great, and awful stillness that was like the stillness of Death. The Earth was a place of gloom, and mist, where spectral shadows writhed, and twisted, and flitted under a frowning heaven, and out of the gloom there came a breath, sharp, and damp, and exceeding chill.

Therefore, as Bellew gazed down from the frowning Heaven to the gloom of Earth, below, with its ever-moving, misty shapes, he shivered involuntarily.

In another hour it would be day, and with the day, the gates of Arcadia would open for his departure, and he must go forth to become once more a wanderer, going up and down, and to and fro in the world until his course was run.

And yet it was worth having lived for, this one golden month, and in all his wanderings needs must he carry with him the memory of her who had taught him how deep and high, how wide and infinitely far-reaching that thing called "Love" may really be.

And—Porges!—dear, quaint, Small Porges! where under heaven could he ever find again such utter faith, such pure unaffected loyalty and devotion as throbbed within that small, warm heart? How could he ever bid "Good-bye" to loving, eager, little Small Porges?

And then there was Miss Priscilla, and the strong, gentle Sergeant, and Peterday, and sturdy Adam, and Prudence, and the rosy-cheeked maids. How well they all suited this wonderful Arcadia! Yes, indeed he, and he only, had been out of place, and so—he must go—back to the every-day, matter-of-fact world, but how could he ever say "Good-bye" to faithful, loving Small Porges?

Far in the East the grey streak had brightened, and broadened, and was already tinged with a faint pink that deepened, and deepened, as he watched. Bellew had seen the glory of many a sun-rise in divers wild places of the Earth, and, hitherto, had always felt deep within him, the responsive thrill, the exhilaration of hope new born, and joyful expectation of the great, unknown Future. But now, he watched the varying hues of pink, and scarlet, and saffron, and gold, with gloomy brow, and sombre eyes.

Now presently, the Black-bird who lived in the apple-tree beneath his window, (the tree of the inquisitive turn of mind), this Black-bird fellow, opening a drowsy eye, must needs give vent to a croak, very hoarse and feeble; then, (apparently having yawned prodigiously and stretched himself, wing, and leg), he tried a couple of notes,—in a hesitating, tentative sort of fashion, shook himself,—repeated the two notes,—tried three, found them mellower, and more what the waiting world very justly expected of him; grew more confident; tried four; tried five,—grew perfectly assured, and so burst forth into the full, golden melody of his morning song.

Then Bellew, leaning out from his casement, as the first bright beams of the rising sun gilded the top-most leaves of the tree, thus apostrophised the unseen singer:

"I suppose you will be piping away down in your tree there, old fellow, long after Arcadia has faded out of my life. Well, it will be only natural, and perfectly right, of course,—She will be here, and may, perhaps, stop to listen to you. Now if, somehow, you could manage to compose for me a Song of Memory, some evening when I'm gone,—some evening when She happens to be sitting idle, and watching the moon rise over the upland yonder; if, at such a time, you could just manage to remind her of—me, why—I'd thank you. And so,—Good-bye, old fellow!"

Saying which, Bellew turned from the window, and took up a certain bulging, be-strapped portmanteau, while the Blackbird, (having, evidently, hearkened to his request with much grave attention), fell a singing more gloriously than ever.

Meanwhile, Bellew descended the great, wide stair, soft of foot, and cautious of step, yet pausing once to look towards a certain closed door, and so, presently let himself quietly out into the dawn. The dew sparkled in the grass, it hung in glittering jewels from every leaf, and twig, while, now and then, a shining drop would fall upon him as he passed, like a great tear.

Now, as he reached the orchard, up rose the sun in all his majesty filling the world with the splendour of his coming, —before whose kindly beams the skulking mists and shadows shrank affrighted, and fled utterly away.

This morning, "King Arthur" wore his grandest robes of state, for his mantle of green was thick sewn with a myriad flaming gems; very different he looked from that dark, shrouded giant who had so lately been Conspirator No. Two. Yet, perhaps for this very reason, Bellew paused to lay a hand upon his mighty, rugged hole, and, doing so, turned and looked back at the House of Dapplemere.

And truly never had the old house seemed so beautiful, so quaint, and peaceful as now. It's every stone and beam had become familiar and, as he looked, seemed to find an individuality of its own, the very lattices seemed to look back at him, like so many wistful eyes.

Therefore George Bellew, American Citizen, millionaire, traveller, explorer, and—LOVER, sighed as he turned away, —sighed as he strode on through the green and golden morning, and resolutely—looked back no more.

CHAPTER XXIX

*Of the moon's message to Small Porges, and how he told
it to Bellew—in a whisper*

Bellew walked on at a good pace with his back turned resolutely towards the House of Dapplemere, and thus, as he swung into that narrow, grassy lane that wound away between trees, he was much surprised to hear a distant hail. Facing sharp about he espied a diminutive figure whose small legs trotted very fast, and whose small fist waved a weather-beaten cap.

Bellew's first impulse was to turn, and run. But Bellew rarely acted on impulse; therefore, he set down the bulging portmanteau, seated himself upon it, and taking out pipe and tobacco, waited for his pursuer to come up.

"Oh Uncle Porges!" panted a voice, "you did walk so awful fast, an' I called, an' called, but you never heard. An' now, please,—where are you going?"

"Going," said Bellew, searching through his pockets for a match, "going, my Porges, why—er—for a stroll, to be sure, —just a walk before breakfast, you know."

"But then—why have you brought your bag?"

"Bag!" repeated Bellew, stooping down to look at it, "why— so—I have!"

"Please—why?" persisted Small Porges, suddenly anxious. "Why did you—bring it?"

"Well, I expect it was to—er—to bear me company. But how is it you are out so very early, my Porges?"

"Why, I couldn't sleep, last night, you know, 'cause I kept on thinking, and thinking 'bout the fortune. So I got up—in the middle of the night, an' dressed myself, an' sat in the big chair by the window, an' looked at the Money Moon. An' I stared at it, an' stared at it till a wonderful thing happened,—an' what do you s'pose?"

"I don't know."

"Well,—all at once, while I stared up at it, the moon changed itself into a great, big face; but I didn't mind a bit, 'cause it was a very nice sort of face,—rather like a gnome's face, only without the beard, you know. An' while I looked at it, it talked to me, an' it told me a lot of things,—an' that's how I know that you are—going away, 'cause you are, you know,—aren't you?"

"Why, my Porges," said Bellew, fumbling with his pipe, "why Shipmate, I—since you ask me—I am."

"Yes, I was 'fraid the moon was right," said Small Porges, and turned away. But Bellew had seen the stricken look in his eyes, therefore he took Small Porges in the circle of his big arm, and holding him thus, explained to him how that in this great world each of us must walk his appointed way, and that there must, and always will be, partings, but that also there must and always shall be, meetings:

"And so, my Porges, if we have to say 'Good-bye' now,—the sooner we shall meet again,—some day—somewhere."

But Small Porges only sighed, and shook his head in hopeless dejection.

"Does—she—know you're going,—I mean my Auntie Anthea?"

"Oh yes, she knows, Porges."

"Then I s'pose that's why she was crying so, in the night—"

"Crying?"

"Yes;—she's cried an awful lot lately, hasn't she? Last night, —when I woke up, you know, an' couldn't sleep, I went into her room, an' she was crying—with her face hidden in the pillow, an' her hair all about her—"

"Crying!"

"Yes; an' she said she wished she was dead. So then, a course, I tried to comfort her, you know. An' she said 'I'm a dreadful failure, Georgy dear, with the farm, an' everything else. I've tried to be a father and mother to you, an' I've failed in that too,—so now, I'm going to give you a real father,'—an' she told me she was going to marry—Mr. Cassilis. But I said 'No'—'cause I'd 'ranged for her to marry you an' live happy ever after. But she got awful angry again an' said she'd never marry you if you were the last man in the world—'cause she 'spised you so—"

"And that would seem to—settle it!" nodded Bellew gloomily, "so it's 'Good-bye' my Porges! We may as well shake hands now, and get it over," and Bellew rose from the portmanteau, and sighing, held out his hand.

"Oh!—but wait a minute!" cried Small Porges eagerly, "I haven't told you what the Moon said to me, last night—"

"Ah!—to be sure, we were forgetting that!" said Bellew with an absent look, and a trifle wearily.

"Why then—please sit down again, so I can speak into your

ear, 'cause what the Moon told me to tell you was a secret, you know."

So, perforce, Bellew re-seated himself upon his portmanteau, and drawing Small Porges close, bent his head down to the anxious little face; and so, Small Porges told him exactly what the Moon had said. And the Moon's message, (whatever it was), seemed to be very short, and concise, (as all really important messages should be); but these few words had a wondrous, and magical effect upon George Bellew. For a moment he stared wide-eyed at Small Porges like one awaking from a dream, then the gloom vanished from his brow, and he sprang to his feet. And, being upon his feet, he smote his clenched fist down into the palm of his hand with a resounding smack.

"By heaven!" he exclaimed, and took a turn to and fro across the width of the lane, and seeing Small Porges watching him, caught him suddenly up in his arms, and hugged him.

"And the moon will be at the full, tonight!" said he. Thereafter he sat him down upon his portmanteau again, with Small Porges upon his knee, and they talked confidentially together with their heads very close together and in muffled tones.

When, at last, Bellew rose, his eyes were bright and eager, and his square chin, prominent, and grimly resolute.

"So—you quite understand, my Porges?"

"Yes, yes—Oh I understand!"

"Where the little bridge spans the brook,—the trees are thicker, there."

"Aye aye, Captain!"

"Then—fare thee well, Shipmate! Goodbye, my Porges,—and remember!"

So they clasped hands, very solemnly, Big Porges, and Small Porges, and turned each his appointed way, the one up, the other down, the lane. But lo! as they went Small Porges' tears were banished quite; and Bellew strode upon his way, his head held high, his shoulders squared, like one in whom Hope has been newborn.

CHAPTER XXX

How Anthea gave her promise

"And so—he—has really gone!" Miss Priscilla sighed as she spoke, and looked up from her needle-work to watch Anthea who sat biting her pen, and frowning down at the blank sheet of paper before her. "And so, he is—really—gone?"

"Who—Mr. Bellew? Oh yes!"

"He went—very early!"

"Yes."

"And—without any breakfast!"

"That was—his own fault!" said Anthea.

"And without even—saying 'Good-bye'!"

"Perhaps he was in a hurry," Anthea suggested.

"Oh dear me, no my dear! I don't believe Mr. Bellew was ever in a hurry in all his life."

"No," said Anthea, giving her pen a vicious bite, "I don't believe he ever was; he is always so—hatefully placid, and deliberate!" and here, she bit her pen again.

"Eh, my dear?" exclaimed Miss Priscilla, pausing with her needle in mid-air, "did you say—hatefully?"

"Yes."

"Anthea!"

"I—hate him, Aunt Priscilla!"

"Eh?—My dear!"

"That was why I—sent him away."

"You—sent him away?"

"Yes."

"But—Anthea—why?"

"Oh Aunt Priscilla!—surely you never—believed in the—fortune? Surely you guessed it was—*his* money that paid back the mortgage,—didn't you, Aunt,—didn't you?"

"Well, my dear—. But then—he did it so very—tactfully, and —and—I had hoped, my dear that—"

"That I should—marry him, and settle the obligation that way, perhaps?"

"Well, yes my dear, I did hope so—"

"Oh!—I'm going to marry—"

"Then why did you send—"

"I'm going to marry Mr. Cassilis—whenever he pleases!"

"Anthea!" The word was a cry, and her needle-work slipped from Miss Priscilla's nerveless fingers.

"He asked me to write and tell him if ever I changed my mind—"

"Oh—my dear! my dear!" cried Miss Priscilla reaching out imploring hands, "you never mean it,—you are all distraught to-day—tired, and worn out with worry, and loss of sleep, —wait!"

"Wait!" repeated Anthea bitterly, "for what?"

"To—marry—him! O Anthea! you never mean it? Think, —think what you are doing."

"I thought of it all last night, Aunt Priscilla, and all this morning, and—I have made up my mind."

"You mean to write—?"

"Yes."

"To tell Mr. Cassilis that you will—marry him?"

"Yes."

But now Miss Priscilla rose, and, next moment, was kneeling beside Anthea's chair.

"Oh my dear!" she pleaded, "you that I love like my own flesh and blood,—don't! Oh Anthea! don't do what can never be undone. Don't give your youth and beauty to one who can never—never make you happy,—Oh Anthea—!"

"Dear Aunt Priscilla, I would rather marry one I don't love than have to live beholden all my days to a man that I—hate!" Now, as she spoke, though her embrace was as ready, and her hands as gentle as ever, yet Miss Priscilla saw that her proud face was set, and stern. So, she presently rose, sighing, and taking her little crutch stick, tapped dolefully away, and left Anthea to write her letter.

And now, hesitating no more, Anthea took up her pen, and wrote,—surely a very short missive for a love-letter. And, when she had folded, and sealed it, she tossed it aside, and laying her arms upon the table, hid her face, with a long, shuddering sigh.

In a little while, she rose, and taking up the letter, went out to find Adam; but remembering that he had gone to Cranbrook with Small Porges, she paused irresolute, and then turned her steps toward the orchard. Hearing voices, she stopped again, and glancing about, espied the Sergeant, and Miss Priscilla. She had given both her hands into the Sergeant's one, great, solitary fist, and he was looking down at her, and she was looking up at him, and upon the face of each, was a great and shining joy.

And, seeing all this, Anthea felt herself very lonely all at once, and, turning aside, saw all things through a blur of sudden tears. She was possessed, also, of a sudden, fierce loathing of the future, a horror because of the promise her letter contained. Nevertheless she was firm, and resolute on her course because of the pride that burned within her.

So thus it was that as the Sergeant presently came striding along on his homeward way, he was suddenly aware of Miss Anthea standing before him; whereupon he halted, and removing his hat, wished her a "good-afternoon!"

"Sergeant," said she, "will you do something for me?"

"Anything you ask me, Miss Anthea, mam,—ever and always."

"I want you to take this letter to—Mr. Cassilis,—will you?"

The Sergeant hesitated unwontedly, turning his hat about and about in his hand, finally he put it on, out of the way.

"Will you, Sergeant?"

"Since you ask me—Miss Anthea mam—I will."

"Give it into his own hand."

"Miss Anthea mam—I will."

"Thank you!—here it is, Sergeant." And so she turned, and was gone, leaving the Sergeant staring down at the letter in his hand, and shaking his head over it.

Anthea walked on hastily, never looking behind, and so, coming back to the house, threw herself down by the open window, and stared out with unseeing eyes at the roses nodding slumberous heads in the gentle breeze.

So the irrevocable step was taken! She had given her promise to marry Cassilis whenever he would, and must abide by it! Too late now, any hope of retreat, she had deliberately chosen her course, and must follow it—to the end.

"Begging your pardon, Miss Anthea mam—!"

She started, and glancing round, espied Adam.

"Oh!—you startled me, Adam,—what is it?"

"Begging your pardon, Miss Anthea, but is it true as Mr. Belloo be gone away—for good?"

"Yes, Adam."

"Why then all I can say is—as I'm sorry,—ah! mortal sorry I be, an' my 'eart, mam, my 'eart likewise gloomy."

"Were you so—fond of him, Adam?"

"Well, Miss Anthea,—considering as he were—the best, good-naturedest, properest kind o' gentleman as ever was; when I tell you as over an' above all this, he could use his fists better than any man as ever I see,—him having knocked me into a dry ditch, though, to be sure I likewise drawed his claret,—begging your pardon, I'm sure, Miss Anthea; all of which happened on account o' me finding him a-sleeping in your 'ay, mam;—when I tell you furthermore, as he treated me ever as a man, an' wern't noways above shaking my 'and, or smoking a pipe wi' me—sociable like; when I tell you as he were the finest gentleman, and properest man as ever I knowed, or heard tell on,—why, I think as the word 'fond' be about the size of it, Miss Anthea mam!" saying which, Adam nodded several times, and bestowed an emphatic backhanded knock to the crown of his hat.

"You used to sit together very often—under the big apple tree, didn't you, Adam?"

"Ah!—many an' many a night, Miss Anthea."

"Did he—ever tell you—much of his—life, Adam?"

"Why yes, Miss Anthea,—told me summat about his travels, told me as he'd shot lions, an' tigers—away out in India, an' Africa."

"Did he ever mention—"

"Well, Miss Anthea?" said he enquiringly, seeing she had paused.

"Did he ever speak of—the—lady he is going to marry?"

"Lady?" repeated Adam, giving a sudden twist to his hat.

"Yes,—the lady—who lives in London?"

"No, Miss Anthea," answered Adam, screwing his hat tighter, and tighter.

"Why—what do you mean?"

"I mean—as there never was no lady, Miss Anthea,—neither up to Lonnon, nor nowhere's else, as I ever heard on."

"But—oh Adam!—you—told me—"

"Ah!—for sure I told ye, but it were a lie, Miss Anthea, —leastways, it weren't the truth. Ye see, I were afraid as you'd refuse to take the money for the furnitur' unless I made ye believe as he wanted it uncommon bad. So I up an' told ye as he'd bought it all on account o' him being matrimonially took wi' a young lady up to Lonnon—"

"And then—you went to—him, and warned him—told him of the story you had invented?"

"I did, Miss Anthea; at first, I thought as he were going to up an' give me one for myself, but, arterwards he took it very quiet, an' told me as I'd done quite right, an' agreed to play the game. An' that's all about it, an' glad I am as it be off my mind at last. Ah' now, Miss Anthea mam, seeing you're that rich—wi' Master Georgy's fortun',—why you can pay back for the furnitur'—if so be you're minded to. An' I hope as you agree wi' me as I done it all for the best, Miss Anthea?"

Here, Adam unscrewed his hat, and knocked out the wrinkles against his knee, which done, he glanced at Anthea:

"Why—what is it, Miss Anthea?"

"Nothing, Adam,—I haven't slept well, lately—that's all"

"Ah, well!—you'll be all right again now,—we all shall,—now the mortgage be paid off,—shan't we, Miss Anthea?"

"Yes, Adam."

"We 'ad a great day—over to Cranbrook, Master Georgy an' me, he be in the kitchen now, wi' Prudence—a-eating of bread an' jam. Good-night, Miss Anthea mam, if you should be wanting me again I shall be in the stables,—Good-night, Miss Anthea!" So, honest, well-meaning Adam touched his forehead with a square-ended finger, and trudged away. But Anthea sat there, very still, with drooping head, and vacant eyes.

And so it was done, the irrevocable step had been taken; she had given her promise! So now, having chosen her course, she must follow it—to the end.

For, in Arcadia, it would seem that a promise is still a sacred thing.

Now, in a while, lifting her eyes, they encountered those of the smiling Cavalier above the mantel. Then, as she looked, she stretched out her arms with a sudden yearning gesture:

"Oh!" she whispered, "if I were only—just a picture, like you."

CHAPTER XXXI

Which, being the last, is, very properly, the longest in the book

In those benighted days when men went abroad cased in steel, and, upon very slight provocation, were wont to smite each other with axes, and clubs, to buffet and skewer each other with spears, lances, swords, and divers other barbarous engines, yet, in that dark, and doughty age, ignorant though they were of all those smug maxims, and excellent moralities with which we are so happily blessed,—even in that unhallowed day, when the solemn tread of the policeman's foot was all unknown, —they had evolved for themselves a code of rules whereby to govern their life, and conduct. Amongst these, it was tacitly agreed upon, and understood, that a spoken promise was a pledge, and held to be a very sacred thing, and he who broke faith, committed all the cardinal sins. Indeed their laws were very few, and simple, easily understood, and well calculated to govern man's conduct to his fellow. In this day of ours, ablaze with learning, and culture,—veneered with a fine civilization, our laws are complex beyond all knowing and expression; man regulates his conduct—to them,—and is as virtuous, and honest as the law compels him to be.

This is the age of Money, and, therefore, an irreverent age; it is also the age of Respectability (with a very large R),—and the policeman's bludgeon.

But in Arcadia—because it is an old-world place where life follows an even, simple course, where money is as scarce as roguery, the old law still holds; a promise once given, is a sacred obligation, and not to be set aside.

Even the Black-bird, who lived in the inquisitive apple tree, understood, and was aware of this, it had been born in him, and had grown with his feathers. Therefore,—though, to be sure, he had spoken no promise, signed no bond, nor affixed his mark to any agreement, still he had, nevertheless, borne in mind a certain request preferred to him when the day was very young. Thus, with a constancy of purpose worthy of all imitation, he had given all his mind, and thought, to the composition of a song with a new theme. He had applied himself to it most industriously all day long, and now, as the sun began to set, he had at last corked it all out,—every note, every quaver, and trill; and, perched upon a look-out branch, he kept his bold, bright eye turned toward a certain rustic seat hard by, uttering a melodious note or two, every now and then, from pure impatience.

And presently, sure enough, he spied her for whom he waited,—the tall, long limbed, supple-waisted creature—whose skin was pink and gold like the peaches and apricots in the garden, and with soft, little rings of hair that would have made such an excellent lining to a nest. From this strictly utilitarian point of view he had often admired her hair, (had this Black-bird fellow), as she passed to and fro among her flowers, or paused to look up at him and listen to his song, or even sometimes to speak to him in her sweet, low voice.

But to-day she seemed to have forgotten him altogether, she did not even glance his way, indeed she walked with bent head, and seemed to keep her eyes always upon the ground.

Therefore the black-bird hopped a little further along the branch, and peered over to look down at her with first one round eye, and then the other, as she sank upon the seat, near by, and leaned her head wearily against the great tree, behind. And thus he saw, upon the pint and gold of her cheek, something that shone, and twinkled like a drop of dew.

If the Black-bird wondered at this, and was inclined to be curious, he sturdily repressed the weakness,—for here was the audience—seated, and waiting—all expectation for him to begin.

So, without more ado, he settled himself upon the bough, lifted his head, stretched his throat, and, from his yellow bill, poured forth a flood of golden melody as he burst forth into his "Song of Memory."

And what a song it was!—so full of passionate entreaty, of tender pleading, of haunting sweetness, that, as she listened, the bright drop quivering upon her lashes, fell and was succeeded by another, and another. Nor did she attempt to check them, or wipe them away, only she sat and listened with her heavy head pillowed against the great tree, while the Blackbird, glancing down at her every now and then with critical eye to mark the effect of some particularly difficult passage, piped surely as he had never done before, until the listener's proud face sank lower and lower, and was, at last, hidden in her hands. Seeing which, the Black-bird, like the true artist he was, fearing an anti-climax, very presently ended his song with a long-drawn, plaintive note.

But Anthea sat there with her proud head bowed low, long after he had retired for the night. And the sun went down, and the shadows came creeping stealthily about her, and the moon began to rise, big and yellow, over the up-land; but Anthea still sat there with her head, once more resting wearily against "King Arthur," watching the deepening shadows until she was roused by Small Porges' hand upon hers and his voice saying:

"Why,—I do believe you're crying, Auntie Anthea, an' why are you here—all alone, an' by yourself?"

"I was listening to the Black-bird, dear,—I never heard him sing quite so—beautifully, before."

"But black-birds don't make people cry,—an' I know you've

been crying—'cause you sound—all quivery, you know."

"Do I, Georgy?"

"Yes,—is it 'cause you feel—lonely?"

"Yes dear."

"You've cried an awful lot, lately, Auntie Anthea."

"Have I, dear?"

"Yes,—an' it—worries me, you know."

"I'm afraid I've been a great responsibility to you, Georgy dear," said she with a rueful little laugh.

"Fraid you have; but I don' mind the 'sponsibility,—'I'll always take care of you, you know!" nodded Small Porges, sitting down, the better to get his arm protectingly about her, while Anthea stooped to kiss the top of his curly head. "I promised my Uncle Porges I'd always take care of you, an' so I will!"

"Yes, dear."

"Uncle Porges told me—"

"Never mind, dear,—don' let's talk of—him."

"Do you still—hate him, then, Auntie Anthea?"

"Hush, dear!—it's very wrong to—hate people."

"Yes, a course it is! Then—perhaps, if you don't hate him any more—you like him a bit,—jest a—teeny bit, you know?"

"Why—there's the clock striking half-past eight, Georgy!"

"Yes, I hear it,—but—do you,—the teeniest bit? Oh! can't you like him jest a bit—for my sake, Auntie Anthea? I'm always trying to please you,—an' I found you the fortune, you know, so now I want you to please me,—an' tell me you like him— for my sake."

"But—Oh Georgy dear!—you don't understand."

"—'cause you see," Small Porges, continued, "after all, I found him for you—under a hedge, you know—"

"Ah!—why did you, Georgy dear? We were so happy— before—he came—"

"But you couldn't have been, you know; you weren't married—even then, so you couldn't have been really happy, you know;" said Small Porges shaking his head.

"Why Georgy—what do you mean?"

"Well, Uncle Porges told me that nobody can live happy—ever after, unless they're married—first. So that was why I 'ranged for him to marry you, so you could *both* be happy, an' all revelry an' joy,—like the fairy tale, you know."

"But, you see, we aren't in a fairy tale, dear, so I'm afraid we must make the best of things as they are!" and here she sighed again, and rose. "Come, Georgy, it's much later than I thought, and quite time you were in bed, dear."

"All right, Auntie Anthea,—only—don't you think it's jest a bit—cruel to send a boy to bed so very early, an' when the moon's so big, an' everything looks so—frightfully fine? 'sides—"

"Well, what now?" she asked, a little wearily as, obedient to his pleading gesture, she sat down again.

"Why, you haven't answered my question yet, you know."

"What question?" said she, not looking at him.

"Bout my—Uncle Porges."

"But Georgy—I—"

"You do like him—jest a bit—don't you?—please?" Small Porges was standing before her as he waited for her answer, but now, seeing how she hesitated, and avoided his eyes, he put one small hand beneath the dimple in her chin, so that she was forced to look at him.

"You do, please,—don't you?" he pleaded.

Anthea hesitated; but, after all,—*He* was gone, and nobody could hear; and Small Porges was so very small; and who could resist the entreaty in his big, wistful eyes? surely not Anthea. Therefore, with a sudden gesture of abandonment, she leaned forward in his embrace, and rested her weary head against his manly, small shoulder:

"Yes!" she whispered.

"Jest as much as you like—Mr. Cassilis?" he whispered back.

"Yes!"

"A—bit more—jest a teeny bit more?"

"Yes!"

"A—lot more,—lots an' lots,—oceans more?"

"Yes!"

The word was spoken, and, having uttered it, Anthea grew suddenly hot with shame, and mightily angry with herself, and would, straightway, have given the world to have it unsaid; the more so, as she felt Small Porges' clasp tighten joyfully, and, looking up, fancied she read something like triumph in his look.

She drew away from him, rather hastily, and rose to her feet.

"Come!" said she, speaking now in a vastly different tone, "it must be getting very late—"

"Yes, I s'pecks it'll soon be nine o'clock, now!" he nodded.

"Then you ought to be in bed, fast asleep instead of talking such—nonsense, out here. So—come along—at once, sir!"

"But, can't I stay up—jest a little while? You see—"

"No!"

"You see, it's such a—magnif'cent night! It feels as though—things might happen!"

"Don't be so silly!"

"Well, but it does, you know."

"What do you mean—what things?"

"Well, it feels—gnomy, to me. I s'pecks there's lots of elves about—hidden in the shadows, you know, an' peeping at us."

"There aren't any elves,—or gnomes," said Anthea petulantly, for she was still furiously angry with herself.

"But my Uncle Porges told me—"

"Oh!" cried Anthea, stamping her foot suddenly, "can't you talk of anyone, or anything but—him? I'm tired to death of him and his very name!"

"But I thought you liked him—an awful lot, an'—"

"Well, I don't!"

"But, you said—"

"Never mind what I said! It's time you were in bed asleep,—so come along—at once, sir!"

So they went on through the orchard together, very silently, for Small Porges was inclined to be indignant, but much more inclined to be hurt. Thus, they had not gone so very far, when he spoke, in a voice that he would have described as—quivery.

"Don't you think that you're—just the teeniest bit—cruel to me, Auntie Anthea?" he enquired wistfully, "after I prayed an' prayed till I found a fortune for you!—don't you, please?" Surely Anthea was a creature of moods, to-night, for, even while he spoke, she stopped, and turned, and fell on her knees, and caught him in her arms, kissing him many times:

"Yes,—yes, dear, I'm hateful to you,—horrid to you! But I don't mean to be. There!—forgive me!"

"Oh!—it's all right again, now, Auntie Anthea, thank you. I only thought you were jest a bit—hard, 'cause it is such a— magnif'cent night, isn't it?"

"Yes dear; and perhaps there are gnomes, and pixies about. Anyhow, we can pretend there are, if you like, as we used to—"

"Oh will you? that would be fine! Then, please, may I go with you—as far as the brook? We'll wander, you know,—I've never wandered with you in the moonlight,—an' I do love to hear the brook talking to itself,—so—will you wander—jest this once?"

"Well," said Anthea, hesitating, "it's very late!—"

"Nearly nine o 'clock, yes! But Oh!—please don't forget that I found a fortune for you—"

"Very well," she smiled, "just this once."

Now as they went together, hand in hand through the moonlight, Small Porges talked very fast, and very much at random, while his eyes, bright, and eager, glanced expectantly towards every patch of shadow,—doubtless in search of gnomes, and pixies.

But Anthea saw nothing of this, heard nothing of the suppressed excitement in his voice, for she was thinking that by now, Mr. Cassilis had read her letter,—that he might, even then, be on his way to Dapplemere. She even fancied, once or twice, that she could hear the gallop of his horse's hoofs. And, when he came, he would want to—kiss her!

"Why do you shiver so, Auntie Anthea, are you cold?"

"No, dear."

"Well, then, why are you so quiet to me,—I've asked you a question—three times."

"Have you dear? I—I was thinking; what was the question?"

"I was asking you if you would be awful frightened s'posing we did find a pixie—or a gnome, in the shadows; an' would you be so very awfully frightened if a gnome—a great, big one, you know,—came jumping out an'—ran off with you,—should you?"

"No!" said Anthea, with another shiver, "No, dear,—I think I should be—rather glad of it!"

"Should you, Auntie? I'm—so awful glad you wouldn't be frightened. A course, I don't s'pose there are gnomes—I mean great, big ones,—really, you know,—but there might be, on a magnif'cent night, like this. If you shiver again Auntie you'll have to take my coat!"

"I thought I heard a horse galloping—hush!"

They had reached the stile, by now, the stile with the crooked, lurking nail, and she leaned there, a while, to listen. "I'm sure I heard something,—away there—on the road!"

"I don't!" said Small Porges, stoutly,—"so take my hand, please, an' let me 'sist you over the stile."

So they crossed the stile, and, presently, came to the brook that was the most impertinent brook in the world. And here, upon the little rustic bridge, they stopped to look down at the sparkle of the water, and to listen to its merry voice.

Yes, indeed to-night it was as impertinent as ever, laughing, and chuckling to itself among the hollows, and whispering scandalously in the shadows. It seemed to Anthea that it was laughing at her,—mocking, and taunting her with—the future. And now, amid the laughter, were sobs, and tearful murmurs, and now, again, it seemed to be the prophetic voice of old Nannie:

"By force ye shall be wooed and by force ye shall be wed, and there is no man strong enough to do it, but him as bears the Tiger Mark upon him!"

The "Tiger Mark!" Alas! how very far from the truth were poor, old Nannie's dreams, after all, the dreams which Anthea had very nearly believed in—once or twice. How foolish it had all been! And yet even now—

Anthea had been leaning over the gurgling waters while all this passed through her mind, but now,—she started at the sound of a heavy foot-fall on the planking of the bridge, behind her, and—in that same instant, she was encircled by a powerful arm, caught up in a strong embrace,—swung from her feet, and borne away through the shadows of the little copse.

It was very dark in the wood, but she knew, instinctively, whose arms these were that held her so close, and carried her so easily—away through the shadows of the wood,—away from the haunting, hopeless dread of the future from which there had seemed no chance, or hope of escape.

And, knowing all this, she made no struggle, and uttered no word. And now the trees thinned out, and, from under her lashes she saw the face above her; the thick, black brows drawn together,—the close set of the lips,—the grim prominence of the strong, square chin.

And now, they were in the road; and now he had lifted her into an automobile, had sprung in beside her, and—they were off, gliding swift, and ever swifter, under the shadows of the trees.

And still neither spoke, nor looked at each other; only she leaned away from him, against the cushions, while he kept his frowning eyes fixed upon the road a-head; and ever the great car flew onward faster, and faster; yet not so fast as the beating of her heart, wherein shame, and anger, and fear, and—another feeling strove and fought for mastery.

But at last, finding him so silent, and impassive, she must needs steal a look at him, beneath her lashes.

He wore no hat, and as she looked upon him,—with his yellow hair, his length of limb, and his massive shoulders, he might have been some fierce Viking, and she, his captive, taken by strength of arm—borne away by force.—By force!

And, hereupon, as the car hummed over the smooth road, it seemed to find a voice,—a subtle, mocking voice, very like the voice of the brook,—that murmured to her over and over again:

"By force ye shall be wooed, and by force ye shall be wed."

The very trees whispered it as they passed, and her heart throbbed in time to it:

"By force ye shall be wooed, and by force ye shall be wed!" So, she leaned as far from him as she might, watching him with frightened eyes while he frowned ever upon the road in front, and the car rocked, and swayed with their going, as they whirled onward through moonlight and through shadow, faster, and faster,—yet not so fast as the beating of her heart wherein was fear, and shame, and anger, and—another feeling, but greatest of all now, was fear. Could this be the placid, soft-spoken gentleman she had known,—this man, with the implacable eyes, and the brutal jaw, who neither spoke to, nor looked at her, but frowned always at the road in front.

And so, the fear grew and grew within her,—fear of the man whom she knew,—and knew not at all. She clasped her hands nervously together, watching him with dilating eyes as the car slowed down,—for the road made a sudden turn, hereabouts.

And still he neither looked at, nor spoke to her; and therefore, because she could bear the silence no longer, she spoke—in a voice that sounded strangely faint, and far-away, and that shook and trembled in spite of her.

"Where are you—taking me?"

"To be married!" he answered, never looking at her.

"You—wouldn't—dare!"

"Wait and see!" he nodded.

"Oh!—but what do—you mean?" The fear in her voice was more manifest than ever.

"I mean that you are mine,—you always were, you always must and shall be. So, I'm going to marry you—in about half-an-hour, by special license."

Still he did not even glance towards her, and she looked away over the country side all lonely and desolate under the moon.

"I want you, you see," he went on, "I want you more than I ever wanted anything in this world. I need you, because without you my life will be utterly purposeless, and empty. So I have taken you—because you are mine, I know it,—Ah yes! and, deep down in your woman's heart, you know it too. And so, I am going to marry you,—yes I am, unless—" and here, he brought the car to a standstill, and turning, looked at her for the first time.

And now, before the look in his eyes, her own wavered, and fell, lest he should read within them that which she would fain hide from him,—and which she knew they must reveal,—that which was neither shame, nor anger, nor fear, but the other feeling for which she dared find no name. And thus, for a long moment, there was silence.

At last she spoke, though with her eyes still hidden:

"Unless!" she repeated breathlessly.

"Anthea,—look at me!"

But Anthea only drooped her head the lower; wherefore, he leaned forward, and—even as Small Porges had done,—set his hand beneath the dimple in her chin, and lifted the proud, un-willing face:

"Anthea,—look at me!"

And now, what could Anthea do but obey?

"Unless," said he, as her glance, at last, met his, "unless you can tell me—now, as your eyes look into mine,—that you love Cassilis. Tell me that, and I will take you back, this very instant; and never trouble you again. But, unless you do tell me that, why then—your Pride shall not blast two lives, if I can help it. Now speak!"

But Anthea was silent, also, she would have turned aside from his searching look, but that his arms were about her, strong, and compelling. So, needs must she suffer him to look down into her very heart, for it seemed to her that, in that moment, he had rent away every stitch, and shred of Pride's enfolding mantle, and that he saw the truth, at last.

But, if he had, he gave no sign, only he turned and set the car humming upon its way, once more.

On they went through the midsummer night, up hill and down hill, by cross-road and bye-lane, until, as they climbed a long ascent, they beheld a tall figure standing upon the top of the hill, in the attitude of one who waits; and who, spying them, immediately raised a very stiff left arm, whereupon this figure was joined by another. Now as the car drew nearer, Anthea, with a thrill of pleasure, recognized the Sergeant standing very much as though he were on parade, and with honest-faced Peterday beside him, who stumped joyfully forward, and,—with a bob of his head, and a scrape of his wooden leg,—held out his hand to her.

Like one in a dream she took the sailor's hand to step from the car, and like one in a dream, she walked on between the soldier and the sailor, who now reached out to her, each, a hand equally big and equally gentle, to aid her up certain crumbling, and time-worn steps. On they went together until they were come to a place of whispering echoes, where lights burned, few, and dim.

And here, still as one in a dream, she spoke those words which gave her life, henceforth, into the keeping of him who stood beside her,—whose strong hand trembled as he set upon her finger, that which is an emblem of eternity.

Like one in a dream, she took the pen, and signed her name, obediently, where they directed. And yet,—could this really be herself,—this silent, submissive creature?

And now, they were out upon the moon-lit road again, seated in the car, while Peterday, his hat in his hand, was speaking to her. And yet,—was it to her?

"Mrs. Belloo, mam," he was saying, "on this here monumentous occasion—"

"Monumentous is the only word for it, Peterday!" nodded the Sergeant.

"On this here monumentous occasion, Mrs. Belloo," the sailor proceeded, "my shipmate, Dick, and me, mam,—respectfully beg the favour of saluting the bride;—Mrs. Belloo, by your leave—here's health, and happiness, mam!" And, hereupon, the old sailor kissed her, right heartily. Which done, he made way for the Sergeant who, after a moment's hesitation, followed suit.

"A fair wind, and prosperous!" cried Peterday, flourishing his hat.

"And God—bless you—both!" said the Sergeant as the car shot away.

So, it was done!—the irrevocable step was taken! Her life and future had passed for ever into the keeping of him who sat so silent beside her, who neither spoke, nor looked at her, but frowned ever at the road before him.

On sped the car, faster, and faster,—yet not so fast as the beating of her heart wherein there was yet something of fear, and shame,—but greatest of all was that other emotion, and the name of it was—Joy.

Now, presently, the car slowed down, and he spoke to her, though without turning his head. And yet, something in his voice thrilled through her strangely.

"Look Anthea,—the moon is at the full, to-night."

"Yes!" she answered.

"And Happiness shall come riding astride the full moon!" he quoted. "Old Nannie is rather a wonderful old witch, after all, isn't she?"

"Yes."

"And then there is—our nephew,—my dear, little Porges! But for him, Happiness would have been a stranger to me all my days, Anthea. He dreamed that the Money Moon spoke to him, and—but he shall tell you of that, for himself."

But Anthea noticed that he spoke without once looking at her; indeed it seemed that he avoided glancing towards her, of set design, and purpose; and his deep voice quivered, now and then, in a way she had never heard before. Therefore, her heart throbbed the faster, and she kept her gaze bent downward, and thus, chancing to see the shimmer of that which was upon her finger, she blushed, and hid it in a fold of her gown.

"Anthea."

"Yes?"

"You have no regrets,—have you?"

"No," she whispered.

"We shall soon be—home, now!"

"Yes."

"And are you—mine—for ever, and always? Anthea, you— aren't—afraid of me any more, are you?"

"No."

"Nor ever will be?"

"Nor—ever will be."

Now as the car swept round a bend, behold yet two other figures standing beside the way.

"Yo ho, Captain!" cried a voice, "Oh—please heave to, Uncle Porges!"

And, forth to meet them, came Small Porges, running. Yet remembering Miss Priscilla, tapping along behind him, he must needs turn back,—to give her his hand like the kindly, small gentleman that he was.

And now—Miss Priscilla had Anthea in her arms, and they were kissing each other, and murmuring over each other, as loving women will, while Small Porges stared at the car, and all things pertaining thereto, more especially, the glaring head-lights, with great wondering eyes.

At length, having seen Anthea, and Miss Priscilla safely stowed, he clambered up beside Bellew, and gave him the word to proceed. What pen could describe his ecstatic delight as he sat there, with one hand hooked into the pocket of Uncle Porges' coat, and with the cool night wind whistling through his curls. So great was it, indeed, that Bellew was constrained to turn aside, and make a wide detour, purely for the sake of the radiant joy in Small Porges' eager face.

When, at last, they came within sight of Dapplemere, and the great machine crept up the rutted, grassy lane, Small Porges sighed, and spoke:

"Auntie Anthea," said he, "are you sure that you are married— nice an'—tight, you know?"

"Yes, dear," she answered, "why—yes, Georgy."

"But you don't look a bit diff'rent, you know,—either of you. Are you quite—sure? 'cause I shouldn't like you to disappoint me,—after all."

"Never fear, my Porges," said Bellew, "I made quite sure of it while I had the chance,—look!" As he spoke, he took Anthea's left hand, drawing it out into the moonlight, so that Small Porges could see the shining ring upon her finger.

"Oh!" said he, nodding his head, "then that makes it all right I s'pose. An' you aren't angry with me 'cause I let a great, big gnome come an' carry you off, are you, Auntie Anthea?"

"No, dear."

"Why then, everything's quite—magnif'cent, isn't it? An' now we're going to live happy ever after, all of us, an' Uncle Porges is going to take us to sail the oceans in his ship,—he's got a ship that all belongs to his very own self, you know, Auntie Anthea,—so all will be revelry an' joy—just like the fairy tale, after all."

And so, at last, they came to the door of the ancient House of Dapplemere. Whereupon, very suddenly, Adam appeared, bare-armed from the stables, who, looking from Bellew's radiant face to Miss Anthea's shy eyes, threw back his head, vented his great laugh, and was immediately solemn again.

"Miss Anthea," said he, wringing and twisting at his hat, "or— I think I should say,—Mrs. Belloo mam,—there ain't no word for it! least-ways not as I know on, nohow. No words be strong enough to tell the J-O-Y—j'y, mam, as fills us—one an' all." Here, he waved his hand to where stood the comely Prudence with the two rosy-cheeked maids peeping over her buxom shoulders.

"Only," pursued Adam, "I be glad—ah! mortal glad, I be,—as 'tis you, Mr. Belloo sir. There ain't a man in all the world, —or—as you might say,—uni-verse, as is so proper as you to be the husband to our Miss Anthea—as was,—not nohow, Mr. Belloo sir. I wish you j'y, a j'y as shall grow wi' the years, an' abide wi' you always,—both on ye."

"That is a very excellent thought Adam!" said Bellew, "and I think I should like to shake hands on it." Which they did, forthwith.

"An' now, Mrs. Belloo mam," Adam concluded, "wi' your kind permission, I'll step into the kitchen, an' drink a glass o' Prue's ale—to your 'ealth, and 'appiness. If I stay here any longer I won't say but what I shall burst out a-singing in your very face, mam, for I do be that 'appy-'earted,—Lord!"

With which exclamation, Adam laughed again, and turning about, strode away to the kitchen with Prudence and the rosy-cheeked maids, laughing as he went.

"Oh my dears!" said little Miss Priscilla, "I've hoped for this, —prayed for it,—because I believe he is—worthy of you, Anthea, and because you have both loved each other, from the very beginning; oh dear me; yes you have! And so, my dears, —your happiness is my happiness and—Oh, goodness me! here I stand talking sentimental nonsense while our Small Porges is simply dropping asleep as he stands."

"Fraid I am a bit tired," Small Porges admitted, "but it's been a magnif'cent night. An' I think, Uncle Porges, when we sail away in your ship, I think, I'd like to sail round the Horn first 'cause they say it's always blowing, you know, and I should love to hear it blow. An' now—Good-night!"

"Wait a minute, my Porges, just tell us what it was the Money Moon said to you, last night, will you?"

"Well," said Small Porges, shaking his head, and smiling, a slow, sly smile, "I don't s'pose we'd better talk about it, Uncle Porges, 'cause, you see, it was such a very great secret; an 'sides,—I'm awful sleepy, you know!" So saying, he nodded slumberously, kissed Anthea sleepily, and, giving Miss Priscilla his hand, went drowsily into the house.

But, as for Bellew it seemed to him that this was the hour for which he had lived all his life, and, though he spoke nothing of this thought, yet Anthea knew it, instinctively,—as she knew why he had avoided looking at her hitherto, and what had caused the tremor in his voice, despite his iron self-control; and, therefore, now that they were alone, she spoke hurriedly, and at random:

"What—did he—Georgy mean by—your ship?"

"Why, I promised to take him a cruise in the yacht—if you cared to come, Anthea."

"Yacht!" she repeated, "are you so dreadfully rich?"

"I'm afraid we are," he nodded, "but, at least, it has the advantage of being better than if we were—dreadfully poor, hasn't it?"

Now, in the midst of the garden there was an old sun-dial worn by time, and weather, and it chanced that they came, and leaned there, side by side. And, looking down upon the dial, Bellew saw certain characters graven thereon in the form of a poesy.

"What does it say, here, Anthea?" he asked. But Anthea shook her head:

"That, you must read for yourself!" she said, not looking at him.

So, he took her hand in his, and, with her slender finger, spelled out this motto.

Time, and youthe do flee awaie, Love, Oh! Love then, whiles ye may.

"Anthea!" said he, and again she heard the tremor in his voice, "you have been my wife nearly three quarters of an hour, and all that time I haven't dared to look at you, because if I had, I must have—kissed you, and I meant to wait—until your own good time. But Anthea, you have never yet told me that you—love me—Anthea?"

She did not speak, or move, indeed, she was so very still that he needs must bend down to see her face. Then, all at once, her lashes were lifted, her eyes looked up into his—deep and dark with passionate tenderness.

"Aunt Priscilla—was quite—right," she said, speaking in her low, thrilling voice, "I have loved you—from the—very beginning, I think!" And, with a soft, murmurous sigh, she gave herself into his embrace.

Now, far away across the meadow, Adam was plodding his homeward way, and, as he trudged, he sang to himself in a harsh, but not unmusical voice, and the words of his song were these:

"When I am dead, diddle diddle, as well may hap
You'll bury me, diddle diddle, under the tap,
Under the tap, diddle diddle, I'll tell you why,
That I may drink, diddle diddle, when I am dry."

ABOUT THE AUTHOR

John Jeffery Farnol (February 10, 1878 – August 9, 1952), was an English author, known for his many romantic novels, some formulaic and set in the English Regency period, and swashbucklers. He with Georgette Heyer founded the Regency romantic genre; one of his first books, The Broad Highway, has been issued in a version edited by Barbara Cartland.

He was born in Aston, Birmingham and brought up in London and Kent. He attended the Westminster Art School, after he had lost his job in a Birmingham metal-working firm. In 1900, he married Blanche Hawley, daughter of the noted New York scenic artist Hughson Hawley; they moved to the United States, where he found work as a scene painter.

The success of his early novels led Farnol to become a professional writer; he returned to England around 1910, and settled on the south coast. He produced around 40 novels and volumes of stories, and some non-fiction and children's books. He died after a long battle with cancer. His last book was completed by his second wife Phyllis (nee Clarke), whom he had married in 1938.

Choose from Thousands of 1stWorldLibrary Classics By

A. M. Barnard
Ada Leverson
Adolphus William Ward
Aesop
Agatha Christie
Alexander Aaronsohn
Alexander Kielland
Alexandre Dumas
Alfred Gatty
Alfred Ollivant
Alice Duer Miller
Alice Turner Curtis
Alice Dunbar
Allen Chapman
Alleyne Ireland
Ambrose Bierce
Amelia E. Barr
Amory H. Bradford
Andrew Lang
Andrew McFarland Davis
Andy Adams
Angela Brazil
Anna Alice Chapin
Anna Sewell
Annie Besant
Annie Hamilton Donnell
Annie Payson Call
Annie Roe Carr
Annonaymous
Anton Chekhov
Archibald Lee Fletcher
Arnold Bennett
Arthur C. Benson
Arthur Conan Doyle
Arthur M. Winfield
Arthur Ransome
Arthur Schnitzler
Arthur Train
Atticus
B.H. Baden-Powell
B. M. Bower
B. C. Chatterjee
Baroness Emmuska Orczy
Baroness Orczy
Basil King
Bayard Taylor
Ben Macomber
Bertha Muzzy Bower
Bjornstjerne Bjornson

Booth Tarkington
Boyd Cable
Bram Stoker
C. Collodi
C. E. Orr
C. M. Ingleby
Carolyn Wells
Catherine Parr Traill
Charles A. Eastman
Charles Amory Beach
Charles Dickens
Charles Dudley Warner
Charles Farrar Browne
Charles Ives
Charles Kingsley
Charles Klein
Charles Hanson Towne
Charles Lathrop Pack
Charles Romyn Dake
Charles Whibley
Charles Willing Beale
Charlotte M. Braeme
Charlotte M. Yonge
Charlotte Perkins Stetson
Clair W. Hayes
Clarence Day Jr.
Clarence E. Mulford
Clemence Housman
Confucius
Coningsby Dawson
Cornelis DeWitt Wilcox
Cyril Burleigh
D. H. Lawrence
Daniel Defoe
David Garnett
Dinah Craik
Don Carlos Janes
Donald Keyhoe
Dorothy Kilner
Dougan Clark
Douglas Fairbanks
E. Nesbit
E. P. Roe
E. Phillips Oppenheim
E. S. Brooks
Earl Barnes
Edgar Rice Burroughs
Edith Van Dyne
Edith Wharton

Edward Everett Hale
Edward J. O'Biren
Edward S. Ellis
Edwin L. Arnold
Eleanor Atkins
Eleanor Hallowell Abbott
Eliot Gregory
Elizabeth Gaskell
Elizabeth McCracken
Elizabeth Von Arnim
Ellem Key
Emerson Hough
Emilie F. Carlen
Emily Bronte
Emily Dickinson
Enid Bagnold
Enilor Macartney Lane
Erasmus W. Jones
Ernie Howard Pie
Ethel May Dell
Ethel Turner
Ethel Watts Mumford
Eugene Sue
Eugenie Foa
Eugene Wood
Eustace Hale Ball
Evelyn Everett-green
Everard Cotes
F. H. Cheley
F. J. Cross
F. Marion Crawford
Fannie E. Newberry
Federick Austin Ogg
Ferdinand Ossendowski
Fergus Hume
Florence A. Kilpatrick
Fremont B. Deering
Francis Bacon
Francis Darwin
Frances Hodgson Burnett
Frances Parkinson Keyes
Frank Gee Patchin
Frank Harris
Frank Jewett Mather
Frank L. Packard
Frank V. Webster
Frederic Stewart Isham
Frederick Trevor Hill
Frederick Winslow Taylor

Friedrich Kerst
Friedrich Nietzsche
Fyodor Dostoyevsky
G.A. Henty
G.K. Chesterton
Gabrielle E. Jackson
Garrett P. Serviss
Gaston Leroux
George A. Warren
George Ade
Geroge Bernard Shaw
George Cary Eggleston
George Durston
George Ebers
George Eliot
George Gissing
George MacDonald
George Meredith
George Orwell
George Sylvester Viereck
George Tucker
George W. Cable
George Wharton James
Gertrude Atherton
Gordon Casserly
Grace E. King
Grace Gallatin
Grace Greenwood
Grant Allen
Guillermo A. Sherwell
Gulielma Zollinger
Gustav Flaubert
H. A. Cody
H. B. Irving
H.C. Bailey
H. G. Wells
H. H. Munro
H. Irving Hancock
H. R. Naylor
H. Rider Haggard
H. W. C. Davis
Haldeman Julius
Hall Caine
Hamilton Wright Mabie
Hans Christian Andersen
Harold Avery
Harold McGrath
Harriet Beecher Stowe
Harry Castlemon
Harry Coghill
Harry Houidini

Hayden Carruth
Helent Hunt Jackson
Helen Nicolay
Hendrik Conscience
Hendy David Thoreau
Henri Barbusse
Henrik Ibsen
Henry Adams
Henry Ford
Henry Frost
Henry James
Henry Jones Ford
Henry Seton Merriman
Henry W Longfellow
Herbert A. Giles
Herbert Carter
Herbert N. Casson
Herman Hesse
Hildegard G. Frey
Homer
Honore De Balzac
Horace B. Day
Horace Walpole
Horatio Alger Jr.
Howard Pyle
Howard R. Garis
Hugh Lofting
Hugh Walpole
Humphry Ward
Ian Maclaren
Inez Haynes Gillmore
Irving Bacheller
Isabel Cecilia Williams
Isabel Hornibrook
Israel Abrahams
Ivan Turgenev
J.G.Austin
J. Henri Fabre
J. M. Barrie
J. M. Walsh
J. Macdonald Oxley
J. R. Miller
J. S. Fletcher
J. S. Knowles
J. Storer Clouston
J. W. Duffield
Jack London
Jacob Abbott
James Allen
James Andrews
James Baldwin

James Branch Cabell
James DeMille
James Joyce
James Lane Allen
James Lane Allen
James Oliver Curwood
James Oppenheim
James Otis
James R. Driscoll
Jane Abbott
Jane Austen
Jane L. Stewart
Janet Aldridge
Jens Peter Jacobsen
Jerome K. Jerome
Jessie Graham Flower
John Buchan
John Burroughs
John Cournos
John F. Kennedy
John Gay
John Glasworthy
John Habberton
John Joy Bell
John Kendrick Bangs
John Milton
John Philip Sousa
John Taintor Foote
Jonas Lauritz Idemil Lie
Jonathan Swift
Joseph A. Altsheler
Joseph Carey
Joseph Conrad
Joseph E. Badger Jr
Joseph Hergesheimer
Joseph Jacobs
Jules Vernes
Julian Hawthrone
Julie A Lippmann
Justin Huntly McCarthy
Kakuzo Okakura
Karle Wilson Baker
Kate Chopin
Kenneth Grahame
Kenneth McGaffey
Kate Langley Bosher
Kate Langley Bosher
Katherine Cecil Thurston
Katherine Stokes
L. A. Abbot
L. T. Meade

L. Frank Baum
Latta Griswold
Laura Dent Crane
Laura Lee Hope
Laurence Housman
Lawrence Beasley
Leo Tolstoy
Leonid Andreyev
Lewis Carroll
Lewis Sperry Chafer
Lilian Bell
Lloyd Osbourne
Louis Hughes
Louis Joseph Vance
Louis Tracy
Louisa May Alcott
Lucy Fitch Perkins
Lucy Maud Montgomery
Luther Benson
Lydia Miller Middleton
Lyndon Orr
M. Corvus
M. H. Adams
Margaret E. Sangster
Margret Howth
Margaret Vandercook
Margaret W. Hungerford
Margret Penrose
Maria Edgeworth
Maria Thompson Daviess
Mariano Azuela
Marion Polk Angellotti
Mark Overton
Mark Twain
Mary Austin
Mary Catherine Crowley
Mary Cole
Mary Hastings Bradley
Mary Roberts Rinehart
Mary Rowlandson
M. Wollstonecraft Shelley
Maud Lindsay
Max Beerbohm
Myra Kelly
Nathaniel Hawthrone
Nicolo Machiavelli
O. F. Walton
Oscar Wilde
Owen Johnson
P.G. Wodehouse
Paul and Mabel Thorne

Paul G. Tomlinson
Paul Severing
Percy Brebner
Percy Keese Fitzhugh
Peter B. Kyne
Plato
Quincy Allen
R. Derby Holmes
R. L. Stevenson
R. S. Ball
Rabindranath Tagore
Rahul Alvares
Ralph Bonehill
Ralph Henry Barbour
Ralph Victor
Ralph Waldo Emmerson
Rene Descartes
Ray Cummings
Rex Beach
Rex E. Beach
Richard Harding Davis
Richard Jefferies
Richard Le Gallienne
Robert Barr
Robert Frost
Robert Gordon Anderson
Robert L. Drake
Robert Lansing
Robert Lynd
Robert Michael Ballantyne
Robert W. Chambers
Rosa Nouchette Carey
Rudyard Kipling
Saint Augustine
Samuel B. Allison
Samuel Hopkins Adams
Sarah Bernhardt
Sarah C. Hallowell
Selma Lagerlof
Sherwood Anderson
Sigmund Freud
Standish O'Grady
Stanley Weyman
Stella Benson
Stella M. Francis
Stephen Crane
Stewart Edward White
Stijn Streuvels
Swami Abhedananda
Swami Parmananda
T. S. Ackland

T. S. Arthur
The Princess Der Ling
Thomas A. Janvier
Thomas A Kempis
Thomas Anderton
Thomas Bailey Aldrich
Thomas Bulfinch
Thomas De Quincey
Thomas Dixon
Thomas H. Huxley
Thomas Hardy
Thomas More
Thornton W. Burgess
U. S. Grant
Upton Sinclair
Valentine Williams
Various Authors
Vaughan Kester
Victor Appleton
Victor G. Durham
Victoria Cross
Virginia Woolf
Wadsworth Camp
Walter Camp
Walter Scott
Washington Irving
Wilbur Lawton
Wilkie Collins
Willa Cather
Willard F. Baker
William Dean Howells
William le Queux
W. Makepeace Thackeray
William W. Walter
William Shakespeare
Winston Churchill
Yei Theodora Ozaki
Yogi Ramacharaka
Young E. Allison
Zane Grey

Lightning Source UK Ltd.
Milton Keynes UK
UKOW052247270212

188033UK00001B/253/A